MIGRATE

LEAVING SAGE SAFELY

amanda sokell

Published by Profit From Order Ltd

First Published 2021

Sevenoaks, United Kingdom

ISBN 978-1-8383614-0-2 (print)
ISBN 978-1-8383614-1-9 (ebook)

Editing by THPeditingServc
Design & typesetting by Josep Book Designs

CONTENTS

WHAT'S GOING ON?

Sarah pulls her hair out. She is reviewing the monthly accounts from the finance team, and once again, they are late. It is nearly the third week after month-end and she's only just got them. The stock figure looks high, and there is no way to see how much stock they have in the warehouse vs at the suppliers. She makes a mental note to find out how the stock figures are put together.

She's aware of supply problems that have impacted sales, however, the high stock levels make her wonder why this is the case; they are clearly over-stocked. Maybe the stock is in the wrong place? The sales team can't see the stock, so perhaps the supply problem isn't real after all.

Concerned the forward contract for US Dollars might be running low, she turns to the creditors to see how much is due to be paid. Of course, there is no way of knowing how much of the figure is for US suppliers, because it has all been amalgamated in a single figure in pounds. With the currency fluctuations currently being experienced, that may or may not be an accurate picture of the true cost of the currency when they next buy some.

She sits back in her chair. She has little visibility of the regional performance or the performance of different product lines. The business is growing fast and this can't go on for much longer. Whilst it seemed like a good option a decade ago, it seems Sage is now past its sell-by-date and the time has come to invest in a new software tool that can give her a better understanding of what's going on in the business.

That's a scary thought. Software isn't her thing, and whilst she has a highly competent finance manager, she's not sure he's ever been through a software change project. It is such a big risk to take for the business right now, and what she can't afford to happen is to lose access to all the data they've built up over the last ten years. Abandoning that and starting from scratch feels like too big a jump.

Sarah's story is common. As recently as a decade ago, if you started a business and asked your accountant to recommend a finance package, the odds are that they suggested Sage. Sage 50 Accounts, previously known as Sage Line 50, has been described in advertising material as "the UK's most popular accounting software" with a startling 90% of accountants recommending it. Sage got its distribution channel spot on. It saturated the accountancy market, providing accountants with everything they needed to recommend the software. And for the accountants, it was an added bonus that all of their clients were using the same software, making their lives far simpler.

Today, if you set up a business, and ask your accountant a similar question, you are more likely to be recommended to use Xero than Sage. Launched in the UK market in 2008, it has now almost reached a similar penetration level with accountants, who are most likely to recommend Xero to new business owners.

Sarah isn't a new business owner, however, she's been in business for over ten years, and Sage is no longer fit for purpose.

If, like Sarah, you've outgrown Sage, you may be experiencing one of a number of limitations.

Stock in different locations

As a business grows, the supply chain gets more complicated. It becomes more sensible to hold stock at various locations, rather than consolidate in a single place. More complex products may result in parts at different locations, or stock held at manufacturers until it is needed.

Sage maintains inventory in only one location. For a business managing stock in multiple locations, this is a big handicap. Inventory in other sites is tracked on spreadsheets, or numerous part codes created to represent the same code in various places. Every time stock is moved from one location to another, the stock is booked out of one code and into another, to ensure visibility.

Multi-currency trading

UK businesses trade internationally and will continue to do so, BREXIT or not. Raw materials and manufacturing are purchased from Hong Kong, China, the Czech Republic, Europe, and around the world. Sales are made internationally in a variety of currencies. Many businesses routinely transact in pound sterling (GBP), US dollars (USD), and the Euro (EUR).

Unless you have the foreign trader module, (standard in Sage 50 Accounts Professional and Client Manager), and it was switched on before any foreign currency trading, it can be difficult to manage currencies in Sage. I've seen numerous examples of companies who trade in foreign currencies where their Sage setup does not properly support currencies. They are unable to hold currency balances for cash or for suppliers and customers. Currency invoices have to be converted into GBP when they are entered, and a separate log maintained which shows the currency amount due. Customer statements can be difficult to produce. Partial payments and different exchange rates wreak havoc with the processing of simple transactions and the visibility of foreign exchange exposure is non-existent. Finance personnel find all manner of ways around the problem, from including the currency price of an item in its description, to hard-coding reports so they look like they are in currency when the underlying data is not.

When raising purchase orders for goods procured from the EU, prices have to be changed on every line because Sage stores the cost of the goods in GBP and cannot store the currency price. This slows down procurement and causes challenges for staff working with margins and procurement.

Inaccurate Margins

With expansion comes complexity. Product costs that were once straight forward, become more complex. The costs of shipping and import duties need to be amalgamated in the margin. Secondary processes need to be incorporated. When stock is purchased at a discount, this needs to be reflected in the stock valuation.

None of this is easy to do within Sage. If stock is purchased at a discount, the standard cost has to be updated before the goods are booked in to ensure the valuation is as accurate as possible. There is no way to apportion the actual costs of shipping and import duties across deliveries, these can only be factored in via an average based on estimates, and built into the standard cost. Any variations to these will only be reflected through careful analysis and manual changes to the standard costs.

It becomes very challenging to know if the product margins reported are real. Do we know that product X is delivering that margin, or could the margin in fact be lower because we've had to air-freight several shipments which are not included in the underlying cost of goods?

Stock Visibility

Companies that have been in business for a decade and are growing well, are frequently supported by a team of sales professionals. These individuals may be office based, or in the field, and will be knocking down doors to share their portfolio with an ever-increasing supply of customers. When you're in a business that sells 'goods,' a key aspect within the sales process is knowing what stock is available to sell, and how long other stock will take to arrive. There is a significant correlation between sales activity and availability of product.

Sage is a financial system. While it has some security elements, enabling different people to access the various parts of the software, it is rare that sales personnel are granted access to see stock. Salespeople, who have no visibility of stock levels and availability, are trying to sell with one hand tied behind their backs.

Fear of the unknown

Most businesses overstay their welcome in Sage. They plod on with it, despite knowing in their heart of hearts that it no longer serves them well. Owners allow themselves to be distracted by the latest product launch, a big new customer, taking orders via the website, and any number of 'more important' considerations. By the time the decision to move has finally been made, it is often several years too late.

One nagging doubt that contributes to this procrastination is concerns over physically moving from one software tool to another. The information built up over many years has value in the business and the thought of abandoning all this and starting over induces fear. Business owners rarely have the level of technical understanding required for such a project, and in companies running Sage, it is uncommon for other team members to have been through the process elsewhere.

Responsibility

As business owners move through the software selection process, to single out the replacement software tool, one aspect that will be considered is data migration. Software partners will share how they will import the company's data into the new software tool. What often comes to light during negotiations is the responsibilities in this crucial process.

Managers will eventually realise that whilst the software partner will handle getting the data into the new software, it is the responsibility of the business to prepare the data in a suitable format first. This is a significant responsibility and one that few managers know how to approach. All too often, this thorny problem gets moved down the priority list and ignored until it is too late.

As Bush states in <u>Transforming Data – Managing the Migration</u>, "Data quality and appropriate data migration programs are the single most common source of cost overruns on [software] implementations."[1]

Why your data is so important

While writing this book, I asked a bunch of people what they love about data. The answers provide insight into why data is so important.

- "Tell stories."
- "Wrangling clarity out of chaos."
- "That it gives clear insight towards a particular process, data is a powerful tool that can change the world. Without data, you only have an opinion."
- "Good data is essential to run and manage a growing business."
- "It facilitates good decision making."
- "Data powers the modern world. It's a valuable commodity - but has interesting characteristics about how to maximize that value: some should be restricted and protected at all costs, and some should be spread as widely as possible. But I don't love data itself - I love what you can do with the right data."

Ask a software partner about their biggest challenges with data migration, and the response could be:

- "Convincing customers of the importance of effective data migration."
- "Getting structured data from clients with no errors."
- "Absence of unique identifiers (or suitable ones at least)."
- "Transformation of the data from one data model to a different data model."
- "Has it all moved across correctly?"
- "Quality assurance."
- "Team members disagreeing on the process for migration."

There is a better way

What business owners may not realise, is data migration is a skill that can be learnt. Rather than forgetting about it and neglecting it, with adequate support, team members can learn effectively how to do it successfully and can ultimately graduate at the end as an accomplished practitioner. To share a great metaphor: "Would you buy a new Lamborghini and put dirty fuel into its tank? Would you expect it to perform as expected? Will you get the full value from this expensive purchase?"[2]

Over two decades, I have worked with companies of all types, from global pharmaceuticals down to five-person family businesses. My experience is deepest with companies who manufacture and have complex parts, bills of material, and sub-assemblies to consider. I have seen different approaches to data migration and the remedy or focus that has, or would have, helped to improve the outcomes. These different practices can be viewed as a hierarchy, which any student of data migration can ascend until they reach the top and become accomplished.

Every year, thousands of companies go through the process of leaving Sage (or another software system). My objective with writing this book is to provide those companies with the knowledge and tools to leave Sage safely, either by

i) getting practical and running the data migration themselves, or

ii) understand what is involved, recognise they need support, and know how best to source, and most importantly, manage that support.

Support may come in the form of engaging the services of a "Functional Data Analyst" or through enrolling in a Data Migration mentoring programme.

CHAPTER ONE

THE LADDER TO ACCOMPLISHED

In order to graduate as accomplished, there are various stages of growth. This is a journey on which multiple team members need to embark. It is rare that a data migration project can be accomplished by a single individual. Including a good number of people in the learning and development programme will provide resilience within the business and ensure the greatest chances of success for the project.

Let's look at the progression ladder.

risk		focus
*	accomplished	standardise
**	organised	rationalise
***	flawed	sanitise
****	haphazard	centralise
*****	neglected	prioritise

seeing the light (accomplished, organised) — *shut in the dark* (flawed, haphazard, neglected)

Figure 1 The Data Migration Progression Ladder

Neglected

"Never neglect details. When everyone's
mind is dulled or distracted the leader
must be doubly vigilant."

— Colin Powell

At **neglected** on the ladder, the data migration is a low priority. The focus is generally on normal business operations, and efforts are going into scoping out the new software with the partner. There will be copious meetings involving all sorts of people, and then when they are back at their desks, they will have the 'day job' with which to contend. Switch-on is many months, hence, who needs to be thinking about the data migration just yet?

In reality, nobody is. It is being neglected. Companies are typically growing, and growth results in a hectic team. Everybody is working hard on day-to-day business operations. The data migration is left at the bottom of a long list of things to do. The fact that, most probably, there is nobody in the business who knows how to approach it, doesn't help. Perhaps it has been given to the finance team to manage, and they don't know where to start.

If your project plan doesn't yet have any data migration tasks, they are all in the future, or they aren't getting done, you are probably on the **neglected** rung of the ladder.

A client with an in-house software development team could have been well placed to handle the data migration. One of its products was software, and with deadlines already over-due, the technical staff were kept focused on building the latest release, and the data migration was neglected. Two weeks before the software was due to switch-over, a large chunk of the development team started on the data migration task. Working over the weekend, the team syphoned the data out of the old software tools and into the new software. This lack of time meant there was no time for the business to review and verify the results. Shortly after the new software was switched-on, business users discovered an abundance of errors in the data and many records that had been moved over in error. Several weeks later, business users were still manually resolving the errors, at a significant opportunity cost to the company.

An abandoned building's condition rapidly deteriorates through neglect. Weeds may grow up and over it. Walls begin to crumble and damp creeps in. To restore it to its former glory will cost far more than the cost of the regular upkeep.

When data migration is being neglected, the antidote is to **prioritise**. This task, which is a crucial project deliverable needs an owner, and a focus, to ensure that it competes for its share of the available resource.

Allowing this task to remain neglected is to put the entire project at risk. Make somebody accountable and ensure agendas of management and operational meetings include data migration as a standing item.

Haphazard

"Improvisation is terribly haphazard."

– Leo Ornstein

There is often a temptation to distribute data migration, giving each team the responsibility for preparing its own files. This **haphazard** approach proves challenging to manage. Spreadsheets of data are created, frequently in different ways throughout the business. Irregular procedures lead to inconsistent data. Some departments make great progress while others struggle to find the time or have the expertise to undertake the task and lag behind. There is little planning, and the rate of progress is affected by chance. If life is quiet, a lot gets done; if life is busy, nothing gets done.

It is rather like rolling a die, knowing you can only move forward when you throw a six. It becomes a game of chance or luck.

A haphazard approach is also inefficient. Inevitably, there will be some duplication of effort. Each team will need to pull together ways to convert current data into the format required in the new software. Each team will end up re-inventing similar wheels. In the worst case, finance may make assumptions on customer account numbering sequences that differ from the way sales are thinking about things. Consequently, different data sets may be fundamentally disconnected when everything is complete.

You are most likely to be at **haphazard** if you haven't appointed somebody internally with an overarching responsibility for the data migration. You might also be at haphazard if that person is struggling to ensure that tasks are completed on time, and doesn't have sufficient authority to ensure resources are allocated to meet the timelines.

When data migration is haphazard, making any prediction as to how much resource is required, what it will cost, and when it will complete is almost impossible.

To resolve a haphazard approach, **centralise** the responsibility. Centralising does not mean that one person undertakes it all. Instead, one person has oversight of everything going on. This person coordinates the rate of progress, communicates decisions over numbering sequences, and ensures all teams understand which approach to take.

Having one person with overall responsibility for managing this side of the project also means they can track progress and alert senior managers if additional resources become necessary.

Flawed

"If a decision-making process is flawed and dysfunctional, decisions will go awry."
— Carly Fiorina

Having centralised oversight of the project, the next challenge on the ladder, is that data is almost always **flawed**.

Flaws are defects that mar the perfection of something. Faults or errors in the data are flaws. Poor quality data comes in many different forms, all of which need addressing. Address fields where countries and postcodes are stored in the wrong areas, making regional and geographic analysis a challenge. Out of date contact names, email addresses, and telephone numbers. Another common issue is a situation whereby customer accounts and contact records are allocated to internal staff contacts, many of whom have left the organisation, and the records were not updated.

Flaws come in other guises. Omission causes defects because information is incomplete. Credit limits aren't recorded for accounts, product attributes that are now desirable have not previously been captured.

The methods can also be flawed. How data is reviewed, verified and syphoned-off may be flawed. A flawed process may lead to unnecessary work, unrealistic resource requirements, and even a risk of overlooking or excluding data that must be included.

At its worst, flawed working practices can result in data getting corrupted as it moves from one software tool to another. Orders may end up on the wrong customer account; customer details may be over-written with those from another company; data integrity is put at risk when the process is flawed.

When I see flawed practice, it feels very much like the team is attempting to complete a jigsaw puzzle without realising that there are missing pieces and somebody has hidden pieces from another puzzle in the box to make it much harder.

Once you've got your data out of the current database into a tabular form (think spreadsheet), you will have a good idea of how many flaws you have to manage. Are there large gaps, are there duplicate lines? Can you see postcodes in the wrong column or phone numbers in the wrong format? Are you seeing data in different formats – some in a spreadsheet, others in text files? Are multiple teams building lists of the same kind of data? If you are answering yes to any of these questions, you've reached **flawed** on the ladder.

To prevent flawed data or a flawed process, we must look to **sanitise**. Firstly, the data must be sanitised, errors cleaned up and gaps filled. While data will never be 100% correct, to start life in new software with flawed data is to jeopardise the very benefits the new software is designed to deliver.

Sanitising the process involves considering how the process is undertaken, and ensuring that it is as clean and robust as is reasonably possible.

Organised

> *"It's pretty scripted on the road: very organised and compartmentalised, and that's the way it has to be with so many people involved in a Stones tour."*
>
> *– Bobby Keys*

As we near the top of the ladder, we move from a position below an imaginary line where those involved in the data migration feel shut in the dark. Below this threshold, the activities are tactical, and without real oversight. Even centralising doesn't go far enough.

To move above the line, and into the light, requires the process to be **organised**. More than having a central person responsible, this involves considering how all the moving parts and people fit together, where the dependencies exist.

Being organised affects the ability to see progress and to visualise and report on this. It provides an understanding of the resources available, and how they are best put to use to achieve the objective.

You'll know you're at **organised** if you know what is complete and what is yet to be finished, if you have a good idea how long tasks will take to complete, and what additional people might be required to complete them. You will have ensured that your approach is organised, having considered the three key aspects covered in this book, strategy, quality, and quantity.

Part of being organised is to **rationalise**. Streamlining all elements, increases organisation. Rationalising resources avoids duplication. If everybody knows their roles, work gets done more quickly and with less effort overall.

Another aspect to organising involves rationalising the data, to make sure it is manageable and there is a business case for all data that forms part of the process. All too often, without this organisation, data that doesn't need to be sanitised ends up being sanitised anyway.

I think about organised in the same way that busy families often use a family planner to keep track of who is doing what, when, and where. In our family, we have a Sunday meeting with the diary where we go through what everybody is up to over the next week, to spot diary clashes and difficulties with the logistics. With sufficient planning, we can usually overcome most challenges.

Accomplished

> *"There are basically two types of people. People who accomplish things, and people who claim to have accomplished things. The first group is less crowded."*
>
> *– Mark Twain*

Imagine the feeling - it's the day you start the switch-over to your new software. You have all of your data ready to go. It's complete, it's clean and you've even tested it in a successful dry run. You've accomplished the goal.

To achieve the goal requires an **accomplished** team. So few data migration projects result in this, to reach this place requires proficient practices. You could safely say your team has graduated with honours if they've got to this point.

You'll know when you've reached this because your software partner will be beside themselves with glee.

An old definition of accomplish is "to provide polish, to perfect." This definition provides a clue as to the final area of focus to reach this goal. If you aspire to reach the top of the ladder and "accomplished," the focus is to **standardise**.

In the same way that standardising on railway gauge in 1845, allowed us to accomplish a national rail network, ensuring consistency of working practices, tools, and resources is required to achieve a successful data migration.

Standardising how data is exported and verified is a crucial requirement. To reduce the risk of errors, everybody involved must be doing this the same way. Either a documented workflow or an automated one, or both is the way to ensure this occurs.

The consistency of resources is also crucial. Standardising the role people perform and their responsibilities will reduce any risk of confusion. Everybody needs to know what is expected of them, and what is not.

Where data needs cleaning, a standard way of doing this is preferred. If operators are to update data, knowing that everybody is doing it the same way will minimise rework and errors.

Standardising drop-down entries and primary keys with clear methodologies and having central lists of these will ensure that where you have distributed data migration activities, everybody is using aligned data and additional work will not be required.

A roadmap to climb the ladder

If after reading this chapter you recognise that you are not yet in the 'accomplished' category, fear not, everything you need to climb to the top of the ladder is laid out here.

The three main aspects we will focus on are:

- Strategy
- Quantity
- Quality

Under strategy, we look at:

- Are you sure you want to do this? Do you need to worry about data migration, and what are the alternatives?
- Automate Everything - how you can get the process standardised
- Ready Steady Go - what you need to consider at switch-over

Concerning Quantity, we consider:

- No place for just in case - how you can work out what data to include and exclude
- People Power - ensure you have the right people available to complete the job
- Legacy Data Access - how much data do you need to store and for how long

And finally, within the quality theme:

- Data Cleaning - ideas on how to clean data as efficiently as possible
- Use Keys to protect data - how to ensure integrity of your data
- Verification - what to look for and how to go about spotting the problems

CHAPTER TWO

ARE YOU SURE YOU WANT TO?

So, you've got yourself a brand new software system. Perhaps right now you're in the process of thinking about which one to use. Maybe you've picked the system, and you're working with a software provider who is doing all the hard work of setting it up just the way you need it to work. Alternatively, maybe you've already bought something, and you've got the task of getting it all set up and off the ground.

Wherever you are on this journey, at some point, you'll need to make decisions about data migration.

What is data migration?

Data migration is the term used to describe the process of extracting data held in one software tool (the legacy tool) and importing it into a new software tool. Data migration is a crucial step in the process of implementing a new software tool, and it is rarely given the priority it deserves. In the lifecycle of a software project, I refer to data migration as the 'syphoning off' stage.

Figure 2 The Software Implementation Lifecycle

I use the term syphoning because it really is a time consuming and slow process, and requires some precision to ensure it is useful.

Data migration is a bit like driving from Kent to the West Country (Cornwall, Devon, or Somerset) on a Friday before a bank holiday weekend. No matter how early you start, or how long you think it's going to take, it takes longer, much longer. Whatever route you've planned, it never works out, you hit roadblocks and congestion and have to change course on the fly, inevitably costing more money, in extra fuel and meal stops.

Depending on the size of your business, and the quality of the data in your legacy tool, you may decide not to do data migration at all, and instead, you will manually enter everything into the new system. Manual data entry can be the right strategy for some if not all of your data.

So, can you get away without migrating any data? The answer is yes, if any of the following are true:

Your current data is such poor quality you would need to review every record anyway

If the quality of your existing data is weak, importing that data into a new tool would be heart-breaking for anybody involved in setting up the new tool. There is something about a brand new software tool that is clean and shiny, and if you're anything like me, you want to ensure the data it contains is clean and sparkling as well. If you have to review the current information for accuracy and completeness, it may well be quicker to either type it from scratch into the data migration template or type it freshly into the new system. Bear in mind, this will take time, so if you adopt this approach, time how long it takes to manually type in 10 records, and then estimate how long it will take to do it all by hand.

A great example of this is 40 different variations of the same delivery address recorded in a legacy tool. With this as the quality sample, the decision was made to get users to enter delivery addresses again in the new tool after go-live.

You have very little data, fewer than 75 customers, products, suppliers

If you have very few records, the effort involved in creating the data extract, creating the data import, cleaning the data, importing, and verifying it, is likely to be longer than simply typing it in by hand. If you have only a few records, embed your training by having your team enter them manually – the added bonus is that they will learn the new software much faster as they do so.

The data you need to put into the new tool doesn't exist in an electronic format

A key reason for buying a new software tool is often that the current one doesn't capture the information we need. We've used up all of the user-defined (custom) fields, and so the information we want to store isn't in the legacy tool. It might be in a spreadsheet somewhere, and sometimes it isn't even there. One good example of this might be the weight of products or the dimension of boxes. If the data you want to bring into the new system does not already exist in an electronic format, entering it into the new system by hand is often the best solution, with the added benefit of providing real-life scenarios for training and testing purposes.

You can afford to gradually populate the new system and switch on at your leisure

If you are planning on doing a parallel run, running both tools at the same time, you can often take your time to populate the new system gradually. If there is no rush, no big bang switch on, and you have people who can enter the historical data over time, this can be a sensible course of action.

Your data is fairly static and is unlikely to change during the process

Static data that doesn't change can be entered well before go-live. It can be created through the testing and training stages of the project and can sit there waiting to be used when the new system is turned on.

You have many people to train and they have time to input data as part of training

There's nothing quite as powerful as training on real data. No, I don't mean training on a live system, I mean training with actual data that people recognise and understand. When we learn something new, something called cognitive dissonance slows down our ability to take on new learning. By using real-world data to learn something new, it reduces the load on the brain and makes it easier for people to learn the new material. If you have a lot of people to train, you can get them to enter your data as part of the training and get them up and running faster at the same time. This strategy does require central coordination of who puts what data into the system so it can still be challenging to manage.

You have an unlimited supply of cheap/ free resource who can do it for you

If you are over-run with interns, students on work experience, or another source of cheap/free labour, it may be more cost-effective to get the data entered manually, rather than trying to do it via data migration. The time spent writing the extract, verifying the data, cleaning it up—importing it into the new system—comes with a significant cost. People power can work out less expensive in the long run.

You can afford to start afresh, leaving your old data in the legacy tool

If the legacy tool is going to remain available – and I would recommend this every time – you might be able to turn on the new tool, move across open transactions, and carry on from there, without the need to move your legacy data across. Provided the old software is still there to reference, some businesses can merely leave their old data where it is and move forward in the new software with a clean slate.

The reality

In reality, there are very few projects where data migration can be avoided altogether. Very few organisations that have grown out of their legacy tool have the resources and people-power to enter data manually or are prepared to leave it languishing in a legacy system.

If you are in the process of trying to single out the right software tool, asking questions about how data migration will occur is a vital part of the selection process. Many software providers who set up and configure systems say that they will import the data for you. It can sometimes sound like they will do your data migration. Rest assured, however, they will expect you to provide them with comprehensive, clean, validated data in a pre-determined format. What they will do is import it into their pristine system.

Your process of extracting data from your legacy tool, getting it into the right shape, cleaning it, and ensuring it meets the new validation rules, is always out of their scope. It is firmly your responsibility and can cause a project to sink or swim if poorly handled.

Some providers don't even offer to import the data for you. Instead, they teach you how to use the imports and pull the data into the system. In these situations, you are even more exposed because you can end up battling with an unfamiliar import tool, validation error messages you don't understand, and may not spot errors in the data.

The most complex data migration project I've ever encountered was moving data into Microsoft Dynamics AX. The arrangement with the software provider was that the client would learn how to do its own data migration – it was rolling the software out to a range of subsidiaries, so bringing the expertise in-house was a sensible commercial decision. The data migration was tortuous, even for a seasoned expert. It felt less like syphoning off the data and more like trying to push water uphill. After switch-on, it became evident that one column of missing data was the culprit for the system not saving any changes to a raft of financial data that was updated at the end of the month by up to 50 project managers. Had the software provider had their eyes on the data migration, it is possible they may have spotted the error.

Still want to go ahead?

Another option available to you is to bring in somebody who can do the data migration for you. Somebody with experience and technical skills that can make it as painless as possible. A good data migration strategy will ensure that your project stays on track, and the data you bring in to your new system is as clean as is humanly possible.

A great place to start is to put together a list of all the data you need in the new system and work out how many records there are – how frequently that data changes, how complex it is, and how important it is to bring historical records into the new system. Something a bit like this:

Data Type	No of Records	Rate of Change	Complexity	History Required
Chart of Accounts	200	2 per year	None	None
Trial Balance	200* each month	2 per year	None	1 Year
Customers	150	10 per month	Multi-currency	Bought in last 3 years
Products	2,500	20 new every 6 months	Multi-language descriptions	All time

This table will help you to identify which data needs migrating and which can be entered manually.

CHAPTER THREE

AUTOMATE EVERYTHING

There are two different ways to do data migration. One is to automate as much as possible; the other is to rely on the manual running of reports and manipulation. The difference between the two approaches is a bit like trying to navigate the journey to the West Country on a bank holiday weekend. One option is to use a co-pilot and a map to try and avoid the congestion; the other is to use a Sat Nav with live traffic updates that can route you around the congestion automatically because it has visibility of what is going on up ahead.

Why automate?

At switch-on, everyone is working against the clock. One software tool is turned off, and until the new software tool contains your data, is verified and switched on, any business activity gets put to one side, and the backlog starts to grow. The switch-over process needs to be quick and easy. For this reason, as much of the data migration process as possible needs to be automated. Automating has several benefits:

- it speeds up the process, and
- it ensures that the process you perfect during your dry run (testing) is replicated completely at switch-over, minimising the risk of errors.

Despite the title of this chapter, there are occasions where automation isn't sensible. Sometimes the volumes of data are small, and the overhead of automating outweighs the time it takes to enter the data manually. Refer to *Chapter Three: Are you sure you want to?* for examples of this.

Automate anything that doesn't lend itself to manual data entry.

So what is automation?

Sage has many reports. You can run these and export the data into Excel. The data you need as part of your migration includes a trial balance (TB), aged debtors, aged creditors, customer lists, product lists, and so on. However, the formatting of these reports rarely makes it easy to populate the import template supplied by the software partner. Although this is one approach, it is probably not the most efficient. The alternative is to connect a spreadsheet directly to the sage database and return the data table without any formatting into a spreadsheet.

ODBC

The technique used to achieve this is to use an Open Database Connection (ODBC).

Sage reports use one of these, so your PC running Sage will already have this setup, and your spreadsheet can be connected to the Sage table using the existing ODBC connection.

If you need help setting this up from scratch, check out the resources in *Appendix - Create an OBDC Connection to Sage*. The beauty of this approach lies in the ability to update the data in the spreadsheet at any point in time by simply right-clicking in the spreadsheet and pressing Refresh. Connecting the spreadsheet in this way is far quicker than running the report manually in Sage, exporting it into Excel, and finally manipulating it to fit the import template.

Data Transformation

Quickly updating the raw data is the first part of the journey. It is, however, rarely in the format required for importing. This data frequently needs to go through a process of modification before transferring it into the new software, which can also be automated.

Take for example VAT rates.
In Sage, these are usually coded T9, T0, T1, etc. while in many other systems, they are allocated descriptive labels such as VAT20, VAT0, NOVAT, and so on.

We need a way to make this data transformation without having to search and replace the data manually. Instead, we can build a mapping table that automatically looks up the Sage value and returns the newly allocated code. This mapping table is likely to be the first of several, and they're likely to be referenced by multiple data imports, so it makes sense to build a single shared spreadsheet to hold all the mapping tables, one sheet per mapping table. Something a bit like this:

Figure 3 Example of Mapping Tables in Spreadsheet Tabs

What does a mapping table look like?

In its purest form, a mapping table is a two-column spreadsheet. The first column contains the list of possible values from Sage; the second column contains the equivalent option in your new software.

Sage VAT Code	New VAT Code
T0	VAT0
T1	VAT20
T9	NOVAT

Sometimes two values in Sage will be mapped to the same new value, and that's okay.

It becomes more tricky if you discover that some of the records that have for example T0 as their VAT code need mapping to one value and the remaining records need mapping to a different value. Faced with this situation, you have two options available:

Option One

You may decide to clean the data in Sage and allocate a new VAT code to one set of the records. For more details see *Chapter Five: Data Cleaning*.

Option Two

Alternatively, you may be able to find a second or third field which becomes part of the key differentiating between the two sets of records. For example, if the records that are T0 with a country of GB need mapping to NO VAT while those with any other country need mapping to EXPORT, you will end up with a four column mapping table:

- Column A - Sage VAT code
- Column B - Country
- Column C - combined key VAT Code - Country (T0-GB)
- Column D - mapped new code.

Multi-column keys start to introduce a more complex Excel formula as you only want the country to be in the combined key if it's GB. To achieve this requires the use of the IF() function in Excel. For examples of how to use this formula see *Appendix - Creating Multi-Key Lookup Tables*.

You then add this combined key to your Sage data extract by adding a column to the right of the table with the same formula as the combined key in the mapping table (i.e. VAT Code - Country).

SAGE VAT Code	Country	Key	Mapped Code
T1	UK	T1-UK	VAT20
T5	UK	T5-UK	VAT05
T0	UK	T0-UK	NOVAT
T0	AUS	T0	EXPORT
T0	USA	T0	EXPORT

The final step is to add a further column to the right of the data table to pull through the mapped value. Use the LOOKUP() formula in Excel to do this. See *Appendix - Using Excel Lookups* for examples of how this would work.

Separate Files for Separate Imports

I usually build one spreadsheet for each data type to be imported. Once I've got the data table from Sage, and added in all the additional columns required to map the old values to the new ones, the final step is to ensure the table contains a key that will link it to other data tables. Keys may be pre-existing or may have to be created.

Pre-existing keys include customer account number; supplier account number; product code or nominal code. You may need to create keys for addresses or contacts.

Sometimes you will see a key in the data spreadsheet which you can't see on the screen in Sage. These hidden keys make it much more straightforward. It is a good idea to use these wherever possible. It is always preferred to adopt a key that already exists and can't be changed, rather than inventing a new one. Creating a new one almost always involves allocating a number at the point of importing the data and linking the spreadsheets manually, which again adds time to the data migration process at switch-over.

I first came across this idea of creating keys manually at switch-on when I was supporting a client who was moving from Sage to Microsoft Dynamics NAV. In discussion with the partner about the data migration strategy, it became evident they had built in time to allocate each contact with an ID manually before the import. I was able to show that I could assign the records with a key automatically by using a hidden ID field in Sage. Doing so reduced their estimate of the switch-over process by a day. At the time, this was a new concept for this particular software partner.

Other Data Sources

I want to pause and say a word about different data sources. Although this is a book about exporting data from Sage, it would be naive to think that companies running Sage have no data in other systems. I've come across Sage plus a host of other systems, many of these being CRM tools.

If you have other software, the approach is the same and Excel can be used to pull data in from many different sources. The most common being Microsoft Access, SQL Server, and OData (a web data access protocol).

A word about Salesforce

If you have data in Salesforce and are moving out and into a new tool, you have an added complication; Salesforce is a case sensitive platform, whereas most software is case insensitive, including Windows.

So what does this mean? In a case sensitive system *a001* and *A001* would be seen as two completely different keys, whereas in a case insensitive system they would be read as the same thing.

As you can imagine, being case sensitive causes a problem when you pull the two records out of the case sensitive system and import them into a case insensitive system such as Excel or many popular ERP systems.

When you import these records, the first entry in the extract will create a new record. When the import reaches the second entry, one of two things will happen; it will generate an error due to a duplicate entry (which is helpful), or it will silently update the existing record, replacing the previously imported record with the details from the second record (which is not helpful).

What are the options if you find yourself in this situation? Firstly, you can change the keys in your existing software, replace those in lowercase with uppercase letters, and where duplicates exist, assign a new code.

Secondly, if you are unable to renumber the data, you can build a mapping table for the affected records with a combined key.

The key will be the source key plus one other distinct field, such as the company name or parts description. You can then allocate a new key which will form the basis of your updated data.

Such a technique becomes more challenging when you find yourself dealing with other tables that only have the ID field, with no name or description in the raw data. You start to have to join tables together before returning the data to your spreadsheet.

Joining Tables

What happens when the data you need for your import don't all exist in one table in Sage? Perhaps you need to pull supplier prices into the same import as product codes. Or you need the customer name in the same import as the customer contacts or addresses?

Again there are multiple ways to solve this depending upon your confidence with building queries.

A query is a request for data or information from a database table or combination of tables. This data may be generated as results returned by Structured Query Language (SQL) or as pictorials, graphs, or complex effects.

If you'd rather stick to Excel formula, you can use multiple sheets in your spreadsheet, linking each one to a different data table in Sage that contains the data you need. Then you amend one of them by adding columns to the right and using a VLOOKUP() function to pull in the extra information from the other Excel sheets. Information on how to use the VLOOKUP() function can be found in the *Appendix - Using Excel Lookups*.

For those who feel more adventurous, the alternative way is to use a join in the query that returns the data from Sage. To do this, you add both (or all relevant) tables into the query editor, create a join between them on the field that links the tables, and then select the elements of data that you need to show in Excel. If you are using a case-sensitive system, this is the only reliable option. For more details on creating queries, check out the resources in *Appendix - Joining Tables in MS Query*.

Building the final import

The final sheet in your spreadsheet will be the import template provided by the software partner. This template dictates the format in which the data must be presented. The final step is to link this sheet to the data table you've created from Sage. Once you've populated the data in the first row of the template, you can copy it down for as many rows as you have data available. The beauty of this approach is that at any point in time, you can open the file, refresh the Sage data and the import template will immediately be updated.

A word of caution

In one project, I inherited a series of data migration spreadsheets from Sage. The worksheets, primarily the aged debtors and creditors had been created by a member of the finance team (who had subsequently left), and the resulting data had been tested and imported successfully to the new software tool. For several weeks I concentrated on getting the remaining extracts finished and tested.

At switch-over, we decided the first import has to be the customer import. For various reasons, this didn't go well and much of the day was spent working out how to re-number customers and delete the duplicates that were in the data import. As we reached the end of the day, the realisation that we'd only imported the customers so far, and we were already a long way behind, started to dawn. The stress was beginning to build. When we finally got to loading the open debtors, we ran the extract and passed it to the business owner to verify. After a couple of hours, the business owner confirmed that the aged debtor list I had exported matched the data in Sage and tied it to the TB.

The software partner imported the data over the weekend and early on Monday morning it was once again verified by the business in the new software tool and approved. After transactions had started to be processed, the accounts receivable clerk was posting receipts on invoices and realised that customers that paid in USD had many open invoices that were showing in GBP. The enormity of the error hit us all. The client would not be able to run customer statements directly from the software until the open invoices have all been paid. When processing bank receipts, a new workflow to handle the currency variations needed to be worked out. There *was no going back. The import was signed off by the business, and substantial work had been completed since, which made reverting to a snapshot very costly. I struggled to work out what went wrong.*

On further investigation of the data imports, I realised the open debtors was referencing a list of customers that was out of date. Instead of using a shared mapping table, the import file had mapping tables in additional sheets to identify currencies. If the lookup didn't find a match, GBP replaced the empty value.

I learnt a valuable lesson that day to ensure that if there is ever a change of personnel in a project, all previously verified imports need to be re-verified.

Eliminating the risks of excel

Even when automating with Excel, the very act of using a spreadsheet means there are still considerable risks of errors. Formulae get out of alignment; lookups get out of date; lines of data are missed when copying down the sheet and records are lost. Data migration using a spreadsheet, albeit a highly automated one, still presents a significant risk of errors.

Using a reporting tool such as Power BI, QlikView or Tableau can overcome many of these challenges. The strategy is the same; create mapping tables and link tables to the Sage source. The added benefits include:

- being able to connect tables from multiple data sources, e.g. Sage and SQL into a single query, removing the need for as many lookups,
- data which automatically grows and shrinks so you're unlikely to miss lines,
- the ability to link to the data you've already imported to look up values, and
- eliminating the risk of copying formula incorrectly and data in one row accidentally being shown on a different row, a common mistake as a result of human error, something almost unavoidable using Excel.

If you decide to take a non-Excel based approach, my suggestion is to use a reporting tool with which you are already familiar, or engage a technical resource on a contract basis to build the reports you need. Trying to learn a new tool for the first time, while running a data migration project is likely to generate more overall risk than is sensible.

Review Questions

1. Where is your current data? E.g. Sage, SQL, Online?
2. Do you have adequate Excel skills internally?
3. What technical skills do you have to build queries?
4. Is any of your data in a case sensitive software?
5. Do you have access to a reporting tool such as Power BI, QlikView, or Tableau?
6. Can you buy in expertise to help you?
7. What mapping do you need to create?

CHAPTER FOUR

NO PLACE FOR JUST IN CASE

How do you pack for a holiday?

Are you a "take the bare minimum, travel light, as long as you've got some money you can always buy what you've forgotten," type, or are you someone that takes far too many clothes and accessories? "Just in case." And then returns home with most of it never having been worn?

When it comes to data migration, there's no place for "just in case." There is an exponential relationship between the volume of data to migrate and the work involved to extract, clean, and import it.

So how do you discriminate?

I've yet to come across a company that has accurately captured the time, and consequently the cost of its data migration. What I do know is, it is a time consuming, resource intensive process. Therefore, it is an expensive process. Even if it is undertaken wholly by your staff, there is the opportunity cost of what they could be doing.

The general rule of thumb is to syphon-off only the data that you absolutely need. There is some data that all companies will need to include, for example:

- nominal ledger codes
- open debtor transactions
- open creditor transactions
- stock balances
- customers with any one of, an open balance, open sales order, or open quote
- suppliers with any one of, an open balance or open purchase order
- stock codes with any one of, an open stock balance, open sales order, open quote, or open purchase order
- un-reconciled bank transactions
- opening trial balance
- open sales orders (not yet shipped)
- open purchase orders (not yet received)
- supplier prices
- customer prices

Quantities Matter

If any of these categories have only a handful of records, it is almost always more productive to enter them manually rather than building an import. Open bank transactions is a good example, with most businesses these days having only a few of these. Only cheques are likely to be unreconciled, and as we use increasingly fewer and fewer of these the likelihood of unreconciled transactions diminishes. Should there be any, manual entry is a far more sensible approach.

Read *Chapter Three: Are you sure you want to?* for more ways to decide if creating an import is a sensible route to take.

> **Note**
>
> *Open sales orders and open purchase orders: After checking the data, frequently you will identify some records that have been shipped or received, for which invoices have not yet been sent or received. Trying to manage this by importing received not invoiced transactions can cause additional complications with data migration which are rarely justified.*

The simplest way to deal with such transactions is to work on the basis that anything shipped or received has also been invoiced. Keep a manual list of which invoices aren't in Sage, and then create a manual sales or purchase invoice for these transactions in the new ERP once you have switched it on.

What else makes sense to syphon off?

Trial Balance (TB)

If you are switching over mid-financial year, at the very least, you will want to migrate the balance sheet TB at the last year-end, plus the monthly movements for each subsequent month.

Furthermore, if you like to report on this year compared to last year, you will need the balance sheet TB at the previous year-end and monthly movements since then. You will have to complete your most recent year-end again in the new software tool after you've switched on.

> **Note**
>
> *If you have already run your year-end in Sage, it will have updated the P&L nominal code balances. You will need to pay careful attention to how this is presented in the database, as Sage can do some strange things and leave you with a TB that doesn't balance to zero.*

In the process of building the TB import from Sage with a year-end completed a few months earlier, I noticed that the TB data extract from the nominal ledger table in Sage didn't balance to zero. Confused, I decided to run a manual TB report in Sage and then cross-referenced each code to identify those where there were discrepancies. It transpired there were a handful of balances showing as debits, which should have been credits. These were only present in data from the previous financial year, and there seemed to be no apparent pattern to it.

Having identified all the affected nominal codes, I build the import by multiplying each line by a factor, either one (or -1 in the case of those affected entries) which reversed the sign on those lines, and I was, therefore, able to get the TB to balance.

Customers

If you've been using Sage for several years, you are likely to have many clients or customers who have not bought from you recently. Maybe they are no longer in business, or perhaps they bought products you no longer sell. When thinking about which customers to import, it's worth remembering the Pareto rule, 80% of your business comes from 20% of your customers.

Before making the final decision to determine which customers to migrate, take into account how recently they've purchased and how frequently they purchase. Establish rules that make sense for your business, and then look at the list of excluded records to double check the logic.

Whatever criteria you come up with, you will also need to include customers that have open balances, open sales orders, or open quotes at the point of switch-over, making this more complicated than it first appears.

> *Reviewing which customers to syphon-off into its new system, the directors of an international design company within the hospitality industry discovered they had 200 customers with five or more invoices within the last 18 months. They decided to use this as the criteria for moving customers. In doing so, they excluded 800 customers who had fewer than five invoices in the same period.*
>
> *The business spent many hours cleaning the data relating to this list of 200 customers. They were credit checked, and credit limits updated, contacts updated and addresses verified. Unfortunately, the selection did not include those with open balances, or unfulfilled sales orders and quotes, and so we had to include additional customers in the import which hadn't been thoroughly cleaned.*

Suppliers

Suppliers require a similar decision, particularly in a business that has been trading for some time. Which suppliers are crucial to the future of the company? Which are no longer required? Think about suppliers who supply your products and components as well as those supplying overheads.

GDPR

I'm sure this isn't the first, and won't be the last book to mention the GDPR, (General Data Protection Regulations) which became law across the EU on the 25th of May 2018. At the time of writing all businesses that trade with citizens located within the EU should have publicised data retention policies - a policy which states for how long the company will store data about individuals. This policy mainly applies after you cease trading with them, as while they are customers or suppliers there is implied consent to store data.

If your data retention policy states that you will keep customer details for no more than three years, you'd better ensure you factor this into your data migration rules. If a customer hasn't purchased from you for three years, you should be removing their data from your system, and certainly not syphoning it off into a new software tool.

Stock Items

There is minimal benefit in moving stock codes that are obsolete and no longer hold stock. Data migration is the perfect opportunity to sell off your old stock. To reduce the number of stock codes you need to syphon-off. To inform your selection, look at how often you order products, and in what quantities. If you don't do an annual review of your product catalogue to retire the ones that make you the least money, now is the time to address this.

Bear in mind that in Sage you may have created stock codes for things for which you don't hold stock as a means of adding charges to orders or invoices. Examples include shipping, packaging, duty, and handling fees. Talk to the new software provider about how best to set these up in the new software, as creating a stock item is unlikely to be the best approach.

Bills of Materials

If you have any form of manufacturing, production, or assembly, you may be using bills of materials (BOMs) to define the components and quantities required to make an item. When you decide to include a stock code, you will also need to add the corresponding BOM. The reverse is also true; if a stock code is in a BOM, you will need to migrate the stock item itself.

Customer Sales History

A big decision to make relates to customer sales history. Wherever possible, if you can manage with only open orders, it will be far more straightforward. Some reasons why you might want more than this include:

- If an order is part-shipped and you will need to be able to show the whole transaction and which parts are outstanding on any customer documentation;
- if you operate monthly and quarterly sales commissions and cannot find an elegant way to ensure you can accurately total the sales from two software tools;
- if you need year-to-date sales reporting and will struggle to accomplish this from two software tools;
- you need to provide customer-facing staff with the ability to see a customer's entire purchase history.

As soon as you decide to migrate historical sales data, your data migration task increases exponentially. It will no longer be possible to cull the customer and stock item codes if you were planning to do so because the chances are you'll find historical data includes stock items you've now retired or customers who no longer buy from you.

One way around this is to map old stock or customers onto a single generic product code or customer such as retired product or legacy customers.

A high-end ladies brand provides a highly personalised shopping experience for its clients in its retail stores. Ladies can walk into any of its five retail stores across two continents and store staff can pull up an entire purchase history. They use this knowledge of what is in the client's wardrobe, to make suggestions from the current season's collection that will coordinate with their existing wardrobe.

When it decided to move from its own Microsoft Access based software tool to a new store Electronic Point of Sale (EPoS) software, it had a decision to make on whether to move the entire sales history or solve the problem a different way.

Being a clothing company, there was an extensive historical catalogue with new clothes being launched into the range twice a year, over 15 years. The prospect of having to include all those redundant codes purely for sales history purposes made this a highly unattractive option.

Instead, they were able to store the historical sales data in an archive against which they built a report showing an individual client's sales history. The migration included historical clients and a

> *button was added to the screen of the new software which ran the statement in a pop-up window for the currently selected customer.*
>
> *This solution gave store personnel instant access to the information they needed, without the headache of moving all that historical data.*

Supplier Sales History

Interestingly, I've rarely been asked to migrate lots of historical supplier data. Whether this is because the focus on growth with my clients is such that their attention is customers and sales trends, or whether this is indicative of a general lack of interest in analysing historical purchasing patterns, I couldn't say.

The arguments are much the same; syphon-off the bare minimum with which you can get away.

Financial Transactions

There is rarely a need to move individual financial transactions. To do so vastly increases the volume of data to be migrated as each operation requires a separate import;

- sales invoices,
- payments on account,
- bank payments,
- journals and so on.

Rather than importing each transaction, ensure your finance team will have access to the historical data to interrogate for at least another two years. With traditional Sage, this is relatively easy to achieve. See *Chapter Eleven: Legacy Data Access* for more details.

Stock Allocations

If you use stock allocations in Sage to allocate stock to sales orders, you will need to consider whether to syphon-off this data as well. If it is essential to honour those sales orders which have effectively been 'promised' inventory and you have transactions processed that have products on backorder, it is worth considering migrating the stock allocations. Factors that might affect this decision include:

- What is the allocation methodology of the new software?
- Will it automatically allocate stock to sales orders?
- If so, on what basis does it assign? By order date or by the date the customer requires the items?
- Does this match the allocation you already have in Sage?

If your new software uses automatic allocation of stock and there is a risk that it might generate a different result from what you already have in Sage and consequently have promised your customers, you may decide to syphon-off your stock allocations and import these.

On the other hand, if you only have a handful of records to allocate and you can have manual stock allocation turned on (albeit temporarily) in your new software, you may choose to run the Sage allocation report and manually make the stock allocations in the new software.

Alternatively, you might be happy to adopt the new methodology for stock allocation, in which case you can ignore this entirely and let the new software allocate the stock according to the rules you have specified.

Contacts

Sage doesn't hold much data on contacts, and many companies use a separate CRM tool to capture rich contact data. This CRM might be Act! Or any one of a host of other CRM options.

When thinking about contact data, the same rules apply. Focus on those contacts that are most recent and most active and consider ignoring the others. Provided you have access to your previous software; you can always look up details for future reference.

Other factors that might affect your choice of contacts to import will be the quality of data versus your new validation rules. A great example of this is email addresses. Many new software tools have inbuilt email validation, which means if you import contacts with missing or invalid email addresses, you will get an error. Unless you are prepared to clean this data painstakingly you may have no choice but to exclude them from the data migration.

Review Questions

1. What is the quality of the data you already have?
2. How different are the validation rules in the new software compared to the existing ones?
3. What is the volume of data cleaning required for each record type?
4. How much data do you really need to move of each type?
5. What factors in the new software tool might affect your data migration?

6. What are alternatives available to you to provide access to historical data without having to migrate it?

7. What are the consequences of extending the range of data on your other data inputs?

CHAPTER FIVE

DATA CLEANING

The quality of data held in most companies' existing software tools is unsatisfactory. Moving to a new software tool represents a golden opportunity to review the current data and have it improved and updated. Even if there is no desire to clean the data, there is often a necessity to enhance data quality because tighter business rules and more sophisticated validation will generate errors during the import process.

A product design organisation that sells internationally reports its entire operation on a regional basis. In moving its data from one system to another, every contact and client needed to have a region based on the country. After reviewing the data, some 22,000 records, it became evident that much of the country information was missing or in the wrong field. To meet its new data validation specifications, all records without a valid country had to be updated.

Make a plan

Given the enormity of such a task having a plan on how it will get done is the first step.

1. Define the data quality rules

During the spell-out phase of your software project, you will define the mandatory fields which must be populated to drive your management reporting. In the previous example, the country is essential because it affects the region, and all reports require the region. There are likely to be a handful of fields that you decide are imperative to run the business. There is often a temptation to make a high number of fields mandatory. However, this can create barriers to software use, and it is advisable to treat mandatory fields with caution.

2. Review the Data

Extract your data in a tabular format so that it is quick and easy to review. For details on how to connect an Excel spreadsheet to your Sage accounts, read *Chapter Four: Automate Everything.*

3. Identify the Changes

Using filters, you can quickly identify the fields that contain gaps or the wrong type of data.

4. Update the Data

The key here is to update the data at the source. So go back into Sage and update the fields with the correct data. This can be done either manually, record by record, or in bulk using the data import facility in Sage.

Start Yesterday

Cleaning data at switch-over is leaving it far too late. Time pressures make this a high-risk strategy and the most successful projects plan their data cleansing well in advance. By the time you get to the final syphon-off, you need to have clean data, or it will slow down the switch-over, ultimately costing you money, if not in fees to the implementation partners, then in more extended downtime.

It's a bit like knowing you're going on holiday and not planning what to take far enough in advance. If you decide to pack on the day of departure, it's highly likely that the clothes you wish to gather will need to be washed and ironed and you no longer have time to do it. When that happens to me, I find myself having to wash clothes as soon as I arrive at the holiday destination, delaying the benefits of the holiday for 24 to 48 hours while they get washed, dried, and ironed.

Can I skip this step?

We can import dirty data into our shiny new software, and when we do we delay the realisation of the benefits until that data is clean. It is often tempting to turn off the data validation solely to get the data into the software. However, that proves frustrating for those using the software, who have to correct all the errors in a record before they can change a single field - a strategy that rarely works.

Identifying the errors

When you have a vast volume of data to review, relying on the human eye to check is risky. Quite apart from the boredom factor in evaluating several thousand records, it is far more reliable and productive to use intelligence tools to find the incorrect data and humans to correct it.

If you've got your data into an Excel spreadsheet, you have many tools at your disposal to find data issues - data that doesn't fit your validation rules. Pivot tables are a fantastic way to dynamically identify records that do not meet data quality rules. If you've never used Pivot tables before, check out the tutorial in the *Appendix - Creating a Pivot Table.*

Pivot Tables

I love pivot tables - I'm a bit of a data geek, so pivot tables excite me due to the way they can help organise and summarise large volumes of data quickly and easily. They are under-utilised in most businesses and have so many applications if you start to think laterally.

To use pivot tables to identify records that need cleaning is relatively straight forward. Add a validation sheet to your spreadsheet and create a pivot table based on your data. Let's say we are looking for any records with a missing county. We would drag the country field up to the top as a page filter and then move the account number and company name into the pivot table as rows.

By filtering the page for blanks, the list of companies with no country will show in the pivot table.

Thus, multiple pivot tables can be created, each one with a different filter to show the records affected by poor quality data in that field.

Complex Criteria

Where we cannot use a single field as a filter, we can use a formula to identify whether validation rules have been met, for example, if you want to check the validity of an email address, you may have to check for multiple exceptions. If the email address doesn't contain an @ sign or doesn't contain a '.', it would be invalid. Additionally, if it includes an '[' or a '<' or a '/' it would be invalid.

We can create a column at the right of our data table which returns TRUE or FALSE based on the above rules. It becomes quite a complicated formula and requires some perseverance to get it right. Once accomplished, the pivot table can be filtered to find all the entries where this value is FALSE. To see an example of the required formula, see *Appendix - Complex Criteria*.

When we have a long drive to achieve, like the one from Kent to Cornwall, there are frequently multiple routes we can choose. While we could manually get out a map and estimate the mileage and travel time of credible alternatives, most of us these days would select a real-time dynamic method to identify possible options, their distance, and journey times. Whether your choice of tool is Google Maps, Waze, or another similar app, these days we rarely rely on humans to process such large volumes of data. The same is true for your data cleaning.

Now that you have several pivot tables identifying the dirty data, you can start to update it in your source system, i.e., Sage. After correcting some records, you can refresh the data, refresh the pivot tables, and check that the list no longer contains the entries. There's something very satisfying about working through an ever-decreasing list.

Duplicate Contacts

Every system... ever... has duplicate contacts or companies — two or more records for the same person or organisation. In Sage, we frequently see multiple accounts for the same customer because the customer requires invoices sent to different addresses. Having two records like this can make credit control very challenging, and having one account with multiple addresses is generally preferred. Sage has no facility to merge accounts and contacts, so how do you ensure your new software doesn't suffer the same affliction?

If you're moving to a software tool that provides you with a tool to merge customers or contacts and there aren't too many of them, it is generally preferable to combine the records in the new software. The advantage of this approach is that the verification process is far more straightforward if the source and destination data are the same.

If your new software cannot merge accounts or you have many clients or contacts to consolidate, it's generally better to combine the records before importing them to the new software.

Merging records can be achieved most easily by building a mapping table for the old account reference with the new one. In this case, the first column contains the Sage Account Number and the second column is the Sage Account number you want it to become. In this way, two different entries in the first column will have the same value in the second column. If you're using Excel, you can use a VLOOKUP() to substitute values in the final import. For further details, see *Chapter Four: Automate Everything*

A professional services client had multiple accounts for Royal Bank of Scotland in its accounts software. Each entry was a different billing address. When it moved to a new software tool, it decided to merge all its Royal Bank of Scotland accounts into a single customer, with multiple addresses. Merging was straightforward

> *until the finance team came to verify the aged debtors, a process*
> *which was more time consuming as numerous outstanding invoices*
> *were now on a different customer.*

Data Cleaning Services

If you have CRM data, you may want to consider using a third-party data cleaning tool. One tool which helps with a high volume of duplicate contacts is Paribus Cloud (www.ParibusCloud.com) which provides a facility to do a one-off de-duplication or an ongoing duplication check.

Address data is frequently poor quality; poor discipline among operators with entering addresses leads to inconsistencies in the data. Postcodes are typed into the county field, counties are missed out, and a whole host of address errors are found in almost any company database. And even if your staff are diligent about entering addresses correctly, the passage of time will render them out of date unless you verify your data regularly. Consumer address data will be affected by deaths, and house moves. Business address date will be affected by business failures. Sadly, the impact of COVID will mean that these numbers will be much higher over the last twelve months than at any time in recent history.

Mailing houses routinely bulk clean address data for customer mailings, and many offer data cleaning as a stand-alone service. Look for the one that holds the ISO 27001 Certification for Information Security Management Systems for a much faster and more cost-effective option where high volumes of data are concerned.

Correcting Data

The most time-consuming aspect of data cleaning is the physical effort required in updating the source data. When faced with updating several thousand records, the sheer effort and mental energy necessary to push through the task often defeats many businesses.

Thankfully, many software tools, including Sage provide facilities to bulk update records, which means that cleaning the data can be done much more quickly. In Sage, you can import via the File menu. Importing allows you to bulk load a file which will create or update records in Sage. It is a powerful tool for your data migration efforts. And it comes with some cautionary considerations:

1. A backup is not optional

Taking a backup of your data before doing a bulk update is not optional, it is necessary. Even the most seasoned professional can make mistakes and having a backup from which you can restore will be essential if something untoward does occur.

2. Minimise the risk

Only include fields you want to update. To reduce the risk of overriding important data by accident, ensure that you include only the fields you want to correct. If, for example, you are populating the country field, add to your input file, two columns, only the account number, and the country.

3. Use keys that match

If your file contains incorrect account codes, the result will be to create lots of new records rather than updating existing ones.

4. You can't import blanks

Sage won't update a field with a blank. If you want to clear an entry in a Sage field, you cannot easily do this with an import. If you don't have anything in a field, the update ignores it. To remove data from a field try instead to replace it with space, " " or a symbol such as an underscore "_" or full stop ".".

> **Note**
>
> *When using symbols in data, avoid at all costs using commas "," which are used to indicate a new field in a comma-separated values (CSV) file; question marks "?" or the asterisk "*", both of which are wild cards used to represent missing letters.*

5. Roll back quickly

If you make a mistake restore Sage. It is always less painful and faster to restore a backup when you've made a mistake. Making the decision quickly, rather than pondering or trying to fix any errors manually, is always the preferred route.

It's a bit like when you take a wrong turn on a car journey; it is nearly always faster to retrace your steps and make the right turn, rather than trying to correct course while continuing to travel in the wrong direction.

Review Questions

1. What fields need to be mandatory?
2. With how few can you get away?
3. What tool will you use to verify the quality of your existing data?
4. Who will be responsible for finding the correct data?

5. How will you update the source with the correct information?
6. How will you merge duplicate records?
7. Who knows how to take backups and restore from one?

CHAPTER SIX

USE KEYS TO PROTECT DATA

One of the challenges with taking a large family group on holiday to the same property is the issue of access. How many keys do you need to provide to ensure that all sub-groups can have independent access during their stay? In our case, we had three different family units all coming and going independently. The owners, however, left only one key, which could have been a challenge to manage.

The owners had an inspired solution; keep the single key in key-safe, the combination of which we all knew. So the key never left the property, and we all knew the algorithm to gain entry while maintaining the security of the property.

When you move data from one software tool to another, the most significant risk is that the keys – or ID fields get corrupted in some way and when the data is re-assembled in the new software tool it has lost its integrity. If you don't protect the keys, you can end up with orders on the wrong customers, contacts on the wrong supplier, balances wrongly assigned, in fact, a total mess.

Accept the Status Quo

The simplest way to avoid any of this from happening is to change nothing. Sage has already assigned keys to your data. Suppliers and customers have account numbers that link all transactions, addresses, and contacts. Stock items have part codes that relate to orders and stock transactions. If you change nothing and move the data 'as is,' you are very unlikely to experience any data corruption.

Multiple Legacy Tools

What if, however, in addition to Sage, you have data in another software tool such as a CRM? It is highly likely that your CRM uses a different key to identify records and how they link together. Possibly you have a field, either in Sage or in the CRM system that connects the two systems.

If you have this scenario, you will need to check that mapping very carefully. Using the techniques outlined in *Chapter Five: Data Cleaning* ensure that you only have a single record in each tool mapped to one other entry in the other software. In installations of this nature, there is rarely any validation over what these 'link' fields can contain, and it is not unusual for duplications to exist, say for example, where multiple companies in the CRM are linked to the same Sage account, or vice-versa. It is crucial to identify these anomalies and fix them before you syphon off any data.

When faced with this scenario, there is another decision to be made. Which key do you use in the new software tool? Many software tools have a facility to use a simple autonumbering sequence when creating new accounts, which is a very different way from the default in Sage. A numbering system can help to highlight how long a customer has been working with you, the most recent will have the highest numbers, and when a company is acquired or changes its name, the account number is still relevant. The Sage default of using letter prefixes based on the name means they can quickly become confusing.

Another consideration to take into account is which system holds the most significant volume of data? If most of the data is in Sage, it may be easier to stick with the Sage ID, however, if most of the transactions are in another (CRM) system, the ID it uses might be more sensible.

A client that used Sage alongside a CRM system undertook the bulk of its activities in the CRM. It was used to store company and contact data, quotes, products, sales orders, purchase orders, stock levels. Sage was only being used to capture the financial transactions in the business. It, therefore, made sense to use the inbuilt IDs in the CRM system as the keys for all the extracts, linking to the equivalent Sage records via a field in the CRM software which stored the corresponding Sage account numbers.

Mind the Gap

One of the challenges clients sometimes face with accepting the idea of using existing auto number keys is a lack of continuity. In short, their order numbers or account numbers don't start at one and increase incrementally without gaps. Records may have been deleted, or you will decide not to bring some data across and will end up with holes in the numbering system. Accept it, and whatever you do, don't try to assign new numbers manually, for you will end up with no end of trouble.

The same client who used Sage alongside a separate CRM system had made significant headway in the data migration process before I became involved. Those responsible had done a pretty good job,

> *with one exception. They hadn't appreciated that the CRM system had an auto number key for each client. Instead, they had decided to abandon the Sage account numbering system in favour of a numerical sequence starting at one. The client had identified about 200 customers it wanted to move across, and so it created a mapping table for each relevant Sage account, assigning a new account number. The problem with this approach is the key that protects data integrity is an entry in a spreadsheet, and as data moves over time, this spreadsheet had to be constantly updated. It also meant that every data extract had to include a Sage account ref link field and then a lookup to find the newly assigned account code.*

This approach adds extra work and complexity to each data set. If you want to keep things simple, wherever possible, avoid manufacturing a key, outside of the software tools you are using.

Keys with Meaning

All sorts of decisions present themselves when moving data from one software tool to another. You will be asked to decide how you want to number all manner of things, customer records, supplier records, sales orders, purchase orders, quotes, invoices are some examples. Deciding the numbering system for new records created in your new software tool is however just part of the process. It would help if you also thought about how you number the data you import and the impact of that on your team that will use the software.

Let's take for example customers. If you decide to adopt an auto numbered system for new records and keep your existing data using an alphanumeric prefix, when you view a list of customers sorted by account number, all the new entries will be sorted at the top, followed by all the customers you have imported. If your new numbering system has a 'C' prefix, for example, they will sort between the B and C records in your existing data.

Alternatively, if you decide to move your existing customers across with a numeric account code, you would be well advised to keep the numbering consistent for new records. Use the same prefix 'C' for all customers and continue the sequence from a number that is higher than the biggest number you migrate.

For example, if the maximum ID in your Sage customer file is C398, you may want to start numbering the next client created in the new software at C400 which is a clear break – helping operators using the system to visually see by the customer account number from which tool it originates.

< 400 Sage vs >= 400 new software.

When you are using a numerical numbering system, you also have to consider how many records you might need to accommodate, to decide on the format of your key. If after ten years of trading, you have 3,000 customers, and you expect growth to continue at a similar rate, in another ten years you can expect to have in the region of 6,000 customers. If your existing numbers go up to 3,059 and you need another 3,000, your numbering system needs to cope with numbers up to 6,059. With a four-digit number, you can create 9,999 records. Consequently, you end up with C0001 - C9999. If you can see a need for more than 10,000 customers, you will need a five-digit format, giving you 99,999 possible records.

When it comes to sales orders, purchase orders, and project codes there is a similar decision to make. Firstly, for what volume of records do you need to allow? How will you ensure your team can quickly identify from which software the data originates? And as these numbers also have an external audience, how will you provide consistency to your outside stakeholders?

A project management client with several business units operated a project numbering scheme within each business unit. Building surveying jobs were in the range 2001+, project management jobs were in the range 9001+, education jobs 5001+, and so on. When considering how to number future jobs in the new software tool, the first big decision taken was to allocate numbers across business units, meaning that the job numbers in any business unit would no longer be consecutive. The second decision made was from what number to start the new numbers, given that many combinations were already in use across all the different business units.

Looking at the existing numbers highlighted that all of the departments were using a four-digit numbering scheme, with one unit using the 9000 numbers range. By going to a five-digit range, all new numbers could start at 10000. This decision provided them with:

- *a clear way to identify whether a project had begun its life in this software or the previous one; and*
- *98,999 potential job records, far more than they would ever use.*

In this way, their job numbers didn't need to change, and external stakeholders saw minimal visual differences on their invoices.

Starting Over

If you decide to restart your numbering sequence in the new system, you also need to think through the consequences of this, let's say you have used over 10,000 sales orders already and instead you want to start new transactions in your new software from one. Most software tools will, by default sort orders and other data alphabetically in ascending order. So, if you've already got order # 9,999 which needs to move across because it is still open, you will want to ensure it sorts above new orders that get created in the new tool. You will also need different prefixes for the two number ranges because otherwise you'll end up recycling numbers and causing confusion and errors.

A client's existing methodology used REF#### for all of its sales orders. The decision was taken to restart the numbering from one, and it wanted to ensure that new transactions were sorted correctly. A CS prefix was added to the Sage orders (creating CSREF###), while the numbering system for new orders became SO###. This approach resulted in the correct sort order as S sorts after C.

Conversely, a different client decided to continue its sales order numbering from its previous software and to add an 'S' prefix to differentiate new orders from older ones. However, during data migration, the existing 'SO' prefix was imported, and once new records started getting created, the 'SO' records always sorted after the 'S' records which meant that the most recent orders always fell in the middle of the list.

A Word on Invoices

Invoice numbers and migrating open invoices deserve a section all of its own. As invoices affect a critical business process—the ability to collect cash from customers—it requires extra careful consideration. There are many pitfalls that are easy to fall into unless you are aware of them in advance.

Invoice numbering sequences are of interest to auditors and clients, and while they follow a predictably incremental pattern, everyone is comfortable. However, if you suddenly send customers invoices with an entirely new numbering system without previously notifying them, you may find some clients contacting you to double check the invoices aren't fraudulent. Auditors also like to understand any gaps in the invoice numbering, so it is worth considering this.

When it comes to migration of open invoices, several factors will determine how easy it is to send customer statements that contain all the information your customers need to settle those invoices.

Invoice Date

The invoice date from Sage may get lost upon import into your new software. If you have many old invoices, to import them with the correct date, your software partner may have to configure accounting periods right back to the date of the first invoice. However, once they've started creating accounting periods, it is often impossible (or very difficult) to open any periods earlier than this. If this happens, they will import your invoices with the invoice date in a field that you can read on the screen, and it is unlikely to be the one that displays on customer statements or informs your aged debt report.

Having a conversation early on about just how old your open invoices are, can prevent this annoying situation.

Invoice Numbers

Invoice numbers are another area where due to the way the new software works it may not be possible to insert your existing sequence into the system, and it will generate a new invoice transaction ID. This transaction ID is the number that is usually visible on customer statements and aged debt reports. Talk to the software provider early in the process to find out how you can ensure your existing invoice numbers can be imported into the new software and display correctly on customer statements and aged debt reports.

Currencies

Invoice currencies are often one of the main reasons why businesses decide to move away from Sage and into another software choice. Sage's inability to handle multi-currency transactions effectively, leaves many companies managing their currency-based invoices in a spreadsheet. If you are moving from Sage to a multi-currency software tool, ensure that you migrate your open invoices (and credits and payments on account) in the right currency, as well as with the same local currency value. If you fail to do this, you will be unable to utilise the automatic customer statement in your new software until all of your old invoices are settled. When this happens, it is such a massive shame because being able to invoice and present statements in the right currency are often some of the main benefits of your new software.

Are you reading this book too late?

Unable to get the open invoice data into your new tool in the right format? It is worth considering whether a bespoke report for aged debtors and customer statements, is required, one which can display the correct Sage data for old invoices, combined with the accurate data from your new software. When making this decision, you should consider the likely time you will have invoices from Sage left unpaid. If you generally clear invoices within a few months it may not be worth having custom reports developed. If on the other hand, you have many very old invoices and this is likely to continue for several months, having a custom report will save much manual manipulation every month.

Review Questions

1. Will you maintain your current ID methodology or change it?
2. If you have multiple software tools, how are they linked?
3. If you link data between multiple software tools, is this data properly clean?
4. Can you use hidden auto numbers to build the keys for your new software?
5. Which of your current software tools holds the most data?
6. What limitations do you have to work around when defining your keys?
7. Are any of these limitations artificial?
8. How will you help software users to know from where a record originates?
9. How much capacity do you need to build into your numbering systems?

10. How will you manage to migrate your open invoices to minimise disruption to your cash collection efforts?

11. How will you communicate any changes to external stakeholders to minimise confusion?

CHAPTER SEVEN

PEOPLE POWER

When faced with a journey of several hours from Kent to Cornwall, the journey time is reduced, and the trip itself is safer when multiple people share the driving. If only one person can drive, the necessity to take rest breaks extends the time, unless safety is compromised. Sharing the driving means that while one driver is resting, another can be making progress on the journey.

Data migration is a team effort. The volume of work involved requires multiple people. It is highly likely that one person will be unable to complete the whole process - from the technical part to extract the data from Sage, to the business sense checking to the laborious process of cleaning the data in the source software.

Alternatively, it is likely to be a full-time role for that one person.

When you start thinking about your data migration, think carefully about the people power involved. Properly resourcing the process will help you to achieve a successful outcome. Who do you need?

Business

The business review of the data is likely to involve multiple people within your organisation. It needs to be people who understand what the data should look like, and its structure in the new software. These people need the following:

- Ability to resolve errors in the current data,
- Understanding of the broader implications of data migration decisions, and
- Ownership and custodian of the business processes affected by the data.

Data Entry

For the task of updating your source systems with clean data, you can use your existing staff - almost anybody can be trained to do this. If like many companies, your team doesn't have sufficient time to focus on this, you can source support elsewhere. Possible options include interns, university students, temporary staff from an agency, work experience for students and even an apprenticeship could be offered to support the entire project. All of these can be very cost-effective ways to manually correct data.

Great candidates for this exhibit:

- High attention to details and accuracy
- High patience levels
- Completer finisher profile

Technical

A crucial part of the syphon-off process involves building the data extracts from Sage, the Excel mapping tables, and the pivot tables to highlight the data that needs cleaning. This role requires a relatively proficient level of both Excel and database query skills. Ideally, you will have somebody on the team who knows how to:

- write SQL queries
- use VLOOKUP formula in Excel
- use the IF, AND, OR functions in Excel
- knows how to concatenate strings in Excel to build multi-field keys

When it comes to updating your Sage data with a batch update, you will need to do this in a controlled manner. Such updates can only be done when nobody is using the software. While not a highly technical role, it does require somebody who is very disciplined and systematic as batch updates on live systems present a high risk of data corruption if undertaken without following a robust process. The best candidates for this task will be:

- familiar with Sage
- have administrative rights
- be thorough and disciplined
- have great attention to detail

Although this is a book about data migration from Sage, experience shows that where Sage exists, there is often a second or third software tool in place which performs other business functions. These software tools, often based on SQL Server, MySQL, or SQL Server Express present more sophisticated methods of updating data. With the right expertise, it can be more efficient to do bulk data updates on the data rather than correcting information manually. Bulk updates require a high level of technical expertise, and anybody doing so, will need experience of:

- making database backups

- restoring a database from a backup
- writing update queries on a subset of data

> A client, running its SQL server-based CRM software decided to exclude from its data migration any companies which had no sensible company name. It was easy enough to write a query that checked for an empty company name and exclude this, however, there were still many records that contained * or ** as the company name. The * is a wildcard, and so it was challenging to include only those records in the selection criteria, and so the decision was made to remove this dirty data and set the names to blanks. Using an update query based on the number of characters in the company name, it was possible to clean hundreds of records in a matter of seconds.

Cautionary Note

Whenever doing bulk updates on a database, a backup must be taken. I recently experienced the panic of a mass update that went wrong. Instead of updating a handful of records, in the middle of a switch-on (time pressures are never conducive to our best work), I updated the entire database. Having over-written the key that linked the database to Sage with a single value for all 20,000 + records, I broke into a hot sweat. Thankfully I had taken a backup and was able to continue the data migration on the copy database. Once the time pressure was over, I used the backup to correct the data in the primary database.

Never enough time

I'm sure I've mentioned this before, and I'll repeat it, this is a highly resource-intensive process. Almost no client has ever accurately recorded the effort required in migrating its data. A recent project offered some insight into the extent of the resource requirements. An outgoing contractor had documented his hours spent building data migration templates and cleaning data, which included 200 customers, a similar number of suppliers, together with their open sales and purchase ledgers.

The time spent totalled 100 hours.

Review Questions

1. What skills do you have in the business?
2. Will you fill any gaps with training or external resource?
3. Who will manage the process?
4. Who owns which data?
5. Does your team have the capacity for this?
6. Will you need to recruit additional resources?
7. What avenues do you have to access inexpensive resources?

CHAPTER EIGHT

VERIFICATION

"The man of science has learned to believe in justification, not by faith, but by verification."

— Thomas Huxley

Satellite navigation is a fantastic invention, and yet it is still fallible. To put blind faith in it is a guarantee that at some point you will get caught out. In the early days of Sat Nav, I remember driving to a meeting with a client on the other side of London. I was running slightly late, and consequently, after punching the postcode into the Sat Nav, rather than visually verifying the route and final destination, I set off. When I arrived at my final destination and couldn't find the office, I then checked the details and realised I'd incorrectly programmed the Sat Nav and was still 20 minutes from where I needed to be.

Verification is one of the least exciting parts of data migration, and yet to ignore it, will leave you open to untold future problems as you discover various mistakes in the data in your brand new software.

Verification requires us to challenge the data we've put together in as many different ways as possible. Its objective is to ensure the accuracy of the data syphoned-off and imported.

Verifying data is a two-step process. The first check happens after you have syphoned-off the data and it is available in a tabular format.

Checking the extract

Get as many people involved in this process as you can; the more people involved, the more errors you'll spot. The nominated business owner is, of course, the most critical person to verify the data at this point.

If you are using an external resource or somebody from a different part of the business to syphon-off your data, your information is just that – data. When they don't work with the data every day, it has no meaning and what might be a glaring error to you will be invisible to them.

In his book Practical Data Migration, Johny Morris identifies some golden rules, one of which is *"Data migration is a business not a technical issue."* The point being that the business, not the technicians, has *"all the experience and expertise to make valid judgements as to the quality and appropriateness of data items."*[3]

> *I wrote an extract of supplier prices for a client. To my eyes, I had produced a bonafide list of products and corresponding rates. However, when the business owner reviewed the extract, they immediately spotted the prices were wrong. It transpired the software stored all the costs in GBP, just like Sage, and they adjusted them for the relevant currency when putting them on a purchase order. The extract needed to be fixed to check the supplier currency and apply the appropriate exchange rate to correct the data.*

Checking the columns

A first pass is to verify that each column of data contains the right kind of information. Have you got words in a field that should be a number? Have you got a number where there should be a date? Has any of the data ended up in the wrong column due to a stray ',' which has split data that should be in one column into two (when saving files as CSV comma separated values an address containing a ',' will push all following fields one column to the right.)

Checking the rows

As you review the rows, you are verifying that your extract has excluded the wrong data and included the right data. If you have chosen to eliminate certain records, you are well-advised to check they are missing from the data source. You also need to check the entries that have been excluded to ensure you haven't caught any records which you need.

Checking dates

Dates are an essential aspect of our business processes. There are order confirmation dates, requested delivery dates, promised dates, shipment dates, expected receipt dates - all manner of dates. Dates drive the customer service experience. Our ability to set expectations for our customers relies on accurate date information. Often when moving from Sage with its limited options into a new software tool, a range of other dates become available and it is essential to understand how you will need to populate these dates to provide useful information. Careful attention to this now will pay huge dividends after you switch on.

Checking Amounts

Being a financial system, it is imperative that any data you move from Sage into a new software tool matches precisely. It will cause all kinds of problems if the value of your sales, stock, or any other financial metric moves during this process. It is therefore imperative to check your numbers against Sage reports before you import them. Your stock balance needs to match the stock valuation report. Your aged debtors and suppliers need to be penny perfect. Open sales orders and purchase orders need to total what is in Sage. Your TB must generate a balance sheet that matches Sage.

When checking amounts, the quickest route is to check the totals, if these are penny perfect, you can generally have confidence that the individual lines will be correct. If you find a difference or want to do a more robust check, you will want to check specific lines. A quick and easy way to achieve this is to export the Sage report to Excel, and then using VLOOKUP() pull the Sage amount into your data extract. By subtracting the Sage amount from the number in your data extract, any difference will be immediately noticeable because the result is not zero.

If you still can't find the error this way, do the VLOOKUP in the opposite direction, pulling the extracted value into the Sage report.

Checking Currencies

One of the key reasons for moving away from Sage is its poor support for currency transactions. Consequently, when verifying your data, you also need to test the entries are in the correct currency, and have the right currency value. Overlooking this check might result in importing GBP transactions rather than the correct transaction currency. It will delay the realisation of a key benefit and require some clunky work processes to work around the error should it happen.

Checking the data in the new software

Any software partner worth its salt will support you with a trial run of importing your data. A trial run, done in conjunction with building the environment for your user acceptance testing is a good strategy. Once they have processed your data, there is another set of checks that need to be completed to ensure the import has been successful.

Total Checking

The first check is to verify that any totals match the original Sage data. Running the corresponding report in your new software tool is the best way to prove this. All financial data can be checked in this manner to quickly get a sense of whether the data import is successful.

Functional Checking

The single most important check that you can do to verify your data import is to run your entire workflow on imported data. Such a test would include:

- booking in stock on an open purchase order
- allocating inventory to an open sales order
- shipping an open sales order
- invoicing the shipment
- transferring stock records or writing them off

- adding information, activities, or quotes to an existing customer
- creating a purchase order for a current supplier
- processing payments on purchase orders
- processing receipts against invoices

Think of as many different scenarios as you can to put your migrated data to the test. Run a full monthly cycle if necessary. You are looking for missing data, incorrect dates or values, fields that contain the wrong information, and ultimately that the software works with the data you've imported. Functional testing is a part of the verification process that receives the least emphasis and priority and yet is the most important. We often spend lots of time testing the system works on new data, and far less time verifying it works on migrated data.

A professional services firm was implementing a significant new ERP software tool. It commissioned a custom forecasting tool interface to ensure its project managers could effectively forecast resources across their projects every month as part of its financial reporting and business planning.

The custom tool was severely delayed and was only delivered a few weeks before the planned switch-on. Despite representations to delay the switch-on to allow for proper testing, there was no appetite to delay the switch on, and so, unfortunately, the data migration and its interaction with the custom forecasting tool was never tested. At the end of the first month of use, 50 project managers each spent many hours updating the forecast for their projects. We ran forecasting clinics with Heroes® chocolates to entice them to come and get help with the process. After much pain and suffering, all project managers had successfully updated their jobs. Roll forward a further month, and again we ran forecasting clinics with chocolate to encourage team members to get their forecasts complete. However, when they opened their projections, it quickly became evident there was a significant issue. While new records created in the new software were as expected, amendments to imported entries did not reflect the changes made the previous month. After a lengthy analysis of the problem, we discovered that the imported forecast records were missing data in one of the columns, that wasn't visible on screen. Due to this missing data, none of the updates had saved, resulting in wasted effort equivalent to about five hours for each of 50 project managers across the two months in question.

Formalising Verification

At switch-over, many partners will require formal sign off before they will import data. If you sign-off your data as ready to go, and after import, it becomes evident there were errors, you may find the partner will charge you to correct the mistakes. The terms of most software implementation contracts will include at least two passes of data import, once as a test and the second at the switch-over. If you then discover errors requiring the data to be re-imported, prepare for a bill for the additional expense.

Should you find yourself in this unfortunate situation, it is almost always faster and cheaper to roll back to a previous version of the database build, before the data set was imported and re-import corrected data. Trying to fix data is almost always slower and therefore more expensive. More information on this can be found in *Chapter Nine: Ready Steady Go.*

Review Questions

1. Who has the expertise to review your business data with meaning?
2. What reports can you reference to verify at a totals level?
3. Do you have the internal expertise to use Excel intelligently to do a line by line verification?
4. Have you written a checklist of what to verify for your team?
5. Have you tested all your data migrations as they appear in your new software?
6. Do you understand the terms of your partner's data migration service?

CHAPTER NINE

READY STEADY GO

When the day finally arrives, and you are ready to switch-over, there are many things you can do to help the data migration run as smoothly as possible. Despite all of these, if you prepare yourself for something to go wrong, you will be ready to respond when it happens.

Have a running list

Before you start, prepare a list of the tasks, in order. Getting the order right is crucial. For example, you can't load sales orders, until you've loaded your products and your customers, as sales orders link to both of these. Work out the order you will import, starting with 'master data' first. Master data includes, your chart of accounts, products, customers, suppliers, locations, addresses, contacts. Some of these can be loaded earlier, provided they aren't going to change before you switch-on.

Complete Month End

Close off as many transactions as possible. If you have to, delay your switch-over until a few days after month-end, and by doing so, you can process all outstanding purchase invoices and shipments and close as many open transactions as possible, it may significantly reduce the extent of your data migration.

- Do you have customers or suppliers with unmatched payments on their accounts? Match them off.
- Do you have obsolete stock sitting in quarantine? Write it off.
- Do you have customers or suppliers with penny balances due to rounding errors? Clear them down.

Use your switch-over as a great reason to thoroughly clean up your data, getting rid of things that have never been a priority.

Complete your month-end before you switch over. Moving data with a clean month-end cut off is always preferable. It provides a static reference point and an audit trail for future reference. If you are unable to complete your month-end before switch-over, recognise that any future adjustments need to be made in both Sage and your new software to ensure full visibility and reconciliation in future. Understanding that you will need to process all these transactions twice can often provide the motivation required to stay late and get the month closed off in record time.

Purchase invoices are often a key sticking point in closing the month early. However, this need not be an issue if an accrual is made to cover them. The extent of the accrual can be estimated before they arrive, or a journal posted in both software tools once the invoices arrive.

VAT Returns

Migrating VAT aware transactions involves a level of complexity that is rarely justified. In an ideal world, you will time your switch-over to co-inside with a VAT period end. If you report VAT monthly, this is less of a concern. Run the VAT return in Sage, and there is no need to make allowances for VAT in your migration. If your switch-over is mid-quarter, it is best not to try to import unreported VAT transactions and then try to run the entire VAT return in your new software. It is far easier to run your VAT report in Sage for the first part of the quarter, run the VAT report in your new software for the rest of the quarter and add all the figures together when completing your return.

Clear Cut Over Dates

When you have identified a suitable cut-off date, ensure this is communicated widely to your team. Make it clear what types of transactions will cease on which dates. Accept that no matter how well you express your cut-off dates, somebody in your organisation will either miss the message or forget and will continue to process data in your existing software. The belt and braces approach to this is to remove all write access to the current software tools to prevent these situations from occurring.

A client ran training on its new software in a testing environment. Staff were encouraged to reinforce that training by completing their weekly timesheets in the test environment until the live switch-on. In the week before switch-on all teams were emailed and reminded that from the following week they would need to use the new, live software and were sent the new URL link.

Two weeks later when missing timesheets came to light, some team members who had not completed their timesheets were chastised for being so tardy. Many of them responded indignity that they had

Removing access to out-of-date environments is the only way to reliability ensure people can't inadvertently use them.

Snapshot Often

Take a snapshot of your Sage system before you start your data migration. When you are ready to syphon-off your data, take a backup of the Sage database. A backup provides you with a static reference point that cannot possibly change.

As you load your data into the new software, take a snapshot after each import. While making a backup takes time and can slow down the data loading timescales, the ability to roll-back to the previous successful import in the event something goes wrong will save you hours in the long run. When taking your backups, it helps to name them "after customers" or "after sales orders" to help quickly identify them. Making a note of the date and time of the backup on your visible progress tracker can also be very helpful.

Make it Visual

Switch-over is a strange time. An entire company staff comes to a form of stasis where it is unable to process business as usual. There is anticipation over verifying extracted data and a sense of being in limbo, wanting to be helpful, and trying to plan their time around when they might be needed to check their set of data. The difficulty for those running the data migration comes from the fact it is almost impossible to estimate how long each step will take and when data will be ready to review. There is an order in which data sets can be prepared and reported which is inflexible due to dependencies in the data. For example, stock balances have to wait until after loading the product codes. Purchase orders rely on suppliers and product codes, and so on.

Providing your team with a visual program check helps everybody to anticipate better when they will be needed, and also helps manage anxious managers who can feel somewhat out of control while the data migration team weaves its magic. Whether you use a white-board in the office or a KanBan-style software tool, the principles are similar.

Firstly, you need a list of all the data imports, which becomes the first column on your whiteboard, or if you decide to use KanBan software such as Trello, becomes the list of cards you need to create in your To-Do channel.

Across the top of your whiteboard, or KanBan board, you need columns for data extracted, extract verified, ready to import, imported, and signed off. When using a whiteboard as each stage is completed, it can be ticked off. The initials of the person responsible can be written into the boxes so they can see where in the process their data has reached.

If using a software tracking tool, cards can be moved from column to column and allocated to people as responsibilities change. Team members will get an automatic email notifying them of the change in the state so they can immediately take action on their step of the process. If you have a distributed team or are working over a weekend, this can be a handy way to both visualise the program and keep everyone in the team up to date.

Allow for Verification

Include verification tasks in your timings. Once you've got your data sets into your new software your team will want to check everything is as expected before they are willing to sign it off. Before you process any further transactions, all migrated data must be signed off by the relevant business owners. No matter how thoroughly you tested and verified the data migration in your test environment, this is the real deal and will be taken much more seriously. Depending on the software and your particular business situation, it may be necessary to put human eyes on each entry to verify it. In this day and age, it still never ceases to surprise me how much manual effort is still required during this part of the process.

> *During the implementation of a project costing software tool for a major professional services firm, the current financial position of each job was moved over from the previous software. The data for each project included time booked in hours and cost, expenses incurred, revenue taken and invoices raised. During testing, it transpired that to build the work in progress entries (revenue – invoicing) each job had to be manually reviewed and an initial transaction posted. With over 1,000 projects in their portfolio, this took over six weeks to complete.*

Have a Plan B

When deciding to switch-over, it also helps to consider your plan B.

The switch-over process is a bit like finally getting into your car to make the long journey down to Cornwall. All the planning you've done cannot prevent the occasional wrong turn that you may take on the trip. When this happens, we have a choice to make. Often the temptation is to continue driving and attempt to correct course as we keep going. We are almost universally reluctant to turn around, retrace our steps, and take the correct turn. The longer it takes us to notice the mistake the less likely we are to switch back and retrace our steps. It is the same when we see an error in our data migration and yet retracing our steps is almost always the faster option.

Nobody likes to go into a software switch-over only to have to resort back to their old software a few days later. Having a plan B that has been thought through and fully understood is however crucial to minimising business risk.

When it comes to the data aspect of this, the trick is to ensure that transactions that need processing in the new software are collected during the downtime at switch-over and clearly identified. After processing in the new software, they need to remain identifiable right up to the point where a roll-back decision has been ruled out.

Roll-back is when you decide that the new software is not acceptable to run the business and despite having processed transactions since switch-on, you feel the company cannot continue to use it. In this situation, you resort back to Sage, re-process the transactions in Sage, and revert to running your business on Sage until such times as the issues that affect your ability to use your new software can be ironed out. At which point you can re-attempt a switch-over.

Having a plan B to roll-back to your previous software includes having a backup to Sage at the point you stopped processing trans-actions and also a backup of your new software before you started loading your live data – i.e. creditors, debtors, stock, sales orders, and purchase orders. When faced with this situation most com-panies will re-attempt the switch-over at the end of the following month. Static data is unlikely to change much in this time, so cus-tomers, suppliers, and product codes that vary only slightly can be left in the new software, reducing the time required to manage the switch-over on the second attempt. Even if you re-run all extracts for completeness, most software imports will recognise existing records and update them, which is generally faster than creating new ones.

Start Clean

At switch-over, make sure your software partner is starting with a clean install and is not working with a database containing previous sets of your data. It may be tempting to run updates on the data at switch-over, for speed purposes. However, if you have refined your keys or eliminated data included in your dry-run, the benefit of starting with a clean database and taking the hit on a slower data load far outweighs the hassle of trying to remove redundant data, manage changes in keys, and generally unpick the mistakes generated by the learning process.

Review Questions

1. What factors influence which month you choose to switch-over?
2. How many days do you need to process month-end?
3. Who is going to reset permissions on Sage to prevent accidental transactions?
4. What spring cleaning can you complete on your data before you syphon-off?
5. Who will be responsible for taking backup snapshots of Sage and other software tools once processing is complete?
6. How will you visualise the process?
7. Which data sets will take the longest to verify?
8. Have you discussed with the software partner their process to ensure you are happy with it?
9. Have you worked out a plan B?

CHAPTER TEN

MIGRATION IS DATA PROCESSING

In May 2018, the General Data Protection Regulations (GDPR) became law. This law affects any business that stores and processes personal data for an individual resident in the EU and (post BREXIT), the UK. Therefore, irrespective of where in the world you are reading this, if your database contains the details of an EU/UK resident (not national), GDPR applies.

As a data controller (an organisation that collects and stores personal data), data migration tasks also need to be compliant within the GDPR. If you store personal data in a system controlled by somebody else, or give another person or organisation access to process the data, they are called a 'data processor.'[4] Personal data is any information that relates to an identified or identifiable individual.[5]

The GDPR sets out some key principles which are relevant to many stages of a data migration project.

Lawfulness, fairness, and transparency[6]

Under this principle, you must have a lawful basis for collecting and using personal data; you must use the personal data in a way that is fair, i.e. you must not process the data in any way that is misleading, unexpected, or unduly detrimental to the individuals concerned;

and you must be clear and honest from the start about how you will use their personal data.

What this means in practice, is that you might want to review your privacy policy. If you name third party systems that you use to store personal data, these may need to be changed. If you decide to store additional information that you haven't previously collected, you will need to revise your privacy policy. Moving from an on-premise system to a cloud-based system is relevant here.

Purpose limitation[7]

You must be clear about how you use people's data from the start and record the purpose in your documentation, obligations, and privacy policy. You can only use data for a new purpose if either this is compatible with your original purpose, you get consent, or you have a clear obligation or function set out in law.

Does your software project have business drivers that are relevant here? Perhaps you've not previously used contact information for marketing purposes? Is a driver for your new system that you will be able to target people with relevant marketing messages? If so, do you have the right consents in place? Do you need to capture people that have not given consent for different types of communication?

Data minimisation[8]

You must ensure that the personal data you are processing is sufficient to fulfil your stated purpose, is relevant to that purpose, and is limited to what is necessary to achieve that purpose.

Have you historically kept information that does not meet this test? Perhaps now is the opportunity to include additional fields to make it sufficient, or to remove some fields that are beyond what is necessary to fulfil your stated purpose?

Accuracy[9]

You should take all reasonable steps to ensure that the data you hold is not incorrect or misleading as to any matter of fact. You need to keep personal data updated, take reasonable steps to correct anything incorrect, and carefully consider any challenges to the accuracy of personal data.

A data migration project represents a golden opportunity to clean up incorrect data. Unfortunately, it is also a potential risk to the accuracy of personal data. It is too easy to corrupt data as it is moved from one system to another, and should this happen, you may find yourself on the wrong side of the law, should that incorrect data subsequently be used to make decisions that might adversely affect an individual. Many of the steps outlined in this book, will help reduce the likelihood of this occurring.

Storage limitation[10]

You must not keep personal data for longer than you need it. You should have a policy statement that describes how long you will hold data and a process for reviewing data and erasing or anonymising it when it is no longer required.

When considering what information to migrate, see *Chapter Four: No place for Just in Case* take notice of your data retention policy. Make sure you don't inadvertently load out-of-date personal data into your new system. If you state you will retain information for four years, and a customer has not bought something for five years, they should not be migrated.

Integrity and confidentiality (security)[11]

You must have the appropriate security measures in place to protect the data you hold.

Concerns here include, who has access to the data? A data migration project generally gives multiple people access to everything in your database. What precautions are you putting in place to ensure those people are keeping the data secure? Is data that normally resides on a server in your office, now sitting in CSV files or spreadsheets for internal review? How are those files secured? Are they on portable devices that may get lost or stolen? The process of moving data from one system to another creates additional challenges that may not be relevant during usual business.

Accountability[12]

This principle requires you to be accountable for what you do with the personal data, and how you comply with the other principles. You must have appropriate records and measures in place to be able to demonstrate your compliance.

It is therefore good practice, at the very least, to ensure that you have confidentially agreements with any third parties involved in your process. This is another opportunity to review current policies and procedures and to ensure that they are still appropriate and relevant within the context of a significant change within your organisation.

Review Questions

1. When was the last time you reviewed your privacy policy and does it now need updating?
2. Have you included a mechanism for recording opt in and opt outs?
3. Are you storing superfluous data?
4. How can you improve the accuracy of personal data?
5. Do your migration criteria align with your privacy policy?
6. How are you protecting data 'in transit'?
7. Have you used confidentiality agreements as required?

CHAPTER ELEVEN

LEGACY DATA ACCESS

So, you've completed a successful switch-on, you're not rolling-back, and everything is going well with the new software. What do you do about your old software? How long do you maintain Sage? How long do you keep your other software tools?

The short answer is as long as possible (subject to your GDPR obligations). Why? Because of human nature to question what doesn't meet our expectations.

When we are using new and unfamiliar tools and habits, we have an inbuilt mistrust of the new world whenever we experience something unexpected. When this happens, our instinctive reaction is to question the new software, the data migration, in fact, everything except our expectation. If we are unable to reassure ourselves using a trusted information source, that we are either correct or incorrect, our confidence and trust of the new world is knocked, and we are more likely to be on the lookout for other evidence to support our position. In this way, confidence in new software can quickly be undermined and can spread rapidly along the internal grapevine.

If you've ever booked a holiday well in advance you may have experienced this phenomenon. Your impression of what to expect is based on your memory of the original advert, which may or may not live up to what you experience when you eventually get there. Without any ability to refer back to the original advert or booking confirmation, you are likely to become very frustrated that the holiday hasn't lived up to expectations. If, however, you have that point of reference, even if it confirms you are mistaken and your expectations were false, you are likely to accept it, move on, and feel more positive about your holiday experience.

Keeping your legacy data available without it costing a fortune to maintain is the crucial factor to examine. Here are some points to consider which will affect your decisions in this area.

For How Long?

For how long do you need access to your old data? Is your business reliant on the same customers for many years, or do you have high levels of churn? If your customer database is out of data quickly, your legacy data will soon become irrelevant.

Generally, financial data needs to be available for HMRC to inspect for up to six years.

By Whom?

How many people will need to access your legacy data? If you have a large team that may need to check back on previous customer orders, it may be necessary to grant them all with access to the data. Alternatively, if this large number of people will rarely need to check data, a single login shared amongst them may suffice.

How?

Can you make the data available in another format – perhaps by running reports which you save as searchable pdf files or read-only excel spreadsheets. For HMRC purposes this would be sufficient, you don't have to keep your records in the original system.

While access to your legacy data is imperative in the short term, business data rapidly becomes out of date, for this reason, it can often be more sensible to extract your data as a series of excel spreadsheets for when you need to refer or report on it in the future.

Compatibility Considerations

Is the software running on your hardware? If you are running software on your equipment and are due to upgrade that hardware shortly, you may discover that your existing software is no longer compatible with the new server, and the cost of an upgrade is not justifiable.

Licencing Considerations

You can maintain a cloud-hosted software like Sage in the Cloud for as long as you wish and are prepared to pay the license fee. You are likely to be able to reduce the number of licenses and share access across your team. Beware of minimum licensing agreements such as minimum terms and minimum users.

What is your licensing model? Is your software licence on a perpetual basis or a monthly or annual basis? Even if you pay a yearly software maintenance charge, you may have a perpetual licence. Historically, Sage was sold with a perpetual licence, which means that once you've purchased it, you can continue to use it without paying any additional money. The annual maintenance and support fee covers you for automatic upgrades and helpdesk support, neither of which you will need. You can confidently cancel this contract and still be able to access your legacy Sage data.

Conversely, if you are on a monthly or annual licencing model, you will need to continue paying your licence fee for as long as you need to be able to access the software. Some software companies charge a monthly fee for their cloud service and also have a non-cloud-based version available either for free or on a perpetual licence. It can be worth switching from the cloud service to an on-premise perpetual licence if you envisage needing the data for a prolonged time.

Trend Reporting

Any business that does long term trend reporting finds the challenge of continuing its trend reporting through a new software implementation a serious consideration.

Often the temptation to move lots of historical data into the new software is simply to satisfy the requirements of its trend reporting. Trend reports tend to work best with two to three years of data, and moving this volume of data is rarely justified.

The trick with this scenario is to be creative with your reporting solution. Reporting tools like Power BI, QlikView, and Tableau can connect to multiple data sources and combine this data into sophisticated trend reports. If you export your legacy data into excel spreadsheets, they can become a data source for your trend reports.

Even if you are using Excel as your reporting tool, it is still possible to create a combined data set from which you can run trend reports. While your Sage data and your new software store data in different formats, the use of lookups and mapping tables can enable you to put mixed data sets into a single table with mapping fields added which will ensure a standard consistent format against which you can report.

A training organisation moved to a new management information system at the end of the academic year. All learners who started their training courses on or after the 1ˢᵗ of August went into the new software. When considering whether or not to migrate their existing learners to the new software, the requirement to generate reports by cohort was a significant factor. Cohorts run from August 1ˢᵗ - July 31ˢᵗ and are determined by when the learner is due to complete their course. Consequently, there is data in the legacy software that needs combining with data created in the new software. This situation is likely to continue for at least 12 months, possibly more, until all those learners complete their courses. At the point of switch-over, the number of learners was in the region of 2,000. Manually moving the data was estimated to take 20 minutes per learner – a total of 95 people days of effort. Another factor in deciding to migrate the data was the annual cost of £5,000 for the licence for the legacy software. However, nine months later, when it would be due for renewal, the number of affected learners was expected to have reduced to 250, a much more achievable task.

In the meantime, to prevent having to move the data, we built a report from the new software, made the legacy report as similar as possible, including blank columns where the data didn't exist to enable both data sets to sit in the same table. Then through the use of additional calculated fields on the right of the data table, populated through mapping tables, the information was harmonised. For example, the legacy software stored M, F and U in the gender field, while the new software stored Male, Female, Refused to Answer. To harmonise this information, a mapping table was created containing all of these possible options and converting it to M, F, and U. The resulting value was then stored in a calculated field at the right of the data table and used in all the reports.

Review Questions

1. Who needs access to your legacy data?
2. For how long is access required?
3. What licencing model do you have?
4. Is your environment compatible with your legacy software?
5. Can you extract the data and store it in a different format?
6. How is your ability to report affected by your data migration?
7. Can you minimise moving data just for reporting purposes through creative reporting strategies?

CHAPTER TWELVE

SEEING THE LIGHT

If you've read this far, it is my hope that you are now in a position to take action.

The range of modern software systems available and the value they can deliver is fundamentally different from what was available even 10-15 years ago. Just 13 years ago, I closed down a bespoke software development company, as I could see the market moving towards off the shelf software that did 90% of what most companies need, without the costs and risks of building something from scratch. In that short time, the software features available to the mid-market business have expanded beyond anything I could have imagined.

And yet, I still see companies battling on with out of date systems, software that they have outgrown, software that doesn't easily integrate, and software that is holding back their people and their company. Systems should provide people and companies with the opportunity to grow and flourish, and where that is not the case, we are sapping the vitality out of our teams and the ability of our companies to profit from technological advances.

If data migration was one of the things holding you back, I hope you now have a better idea of what is involved. If nothing else, it was my desire to remove the cloak of invisibility that shrouds data migration, making it a dark art, to give you a peek into the tasks and considerations required, without having to resort to industry jargon.

I know there will be those who have read this book, who will feel empowered to dive in and manage their data migration projects, all the way up the ladder to organised, and ultimately accomplished. It is inevitable that despite following this process, there will still be things that catch you out, as that is always the way. Even at accomplished, after multiple projects, new things arise, additional complexities need to be considered, so we will forever be students in this field, and that is not a reason to delay further.

I also appreciate that sometimes, showing the inner workings means that suddenly we know what we don't know, and rather than wanting to tread the path to enlightenment ourselves, we would rather hire somebody else to do it. If that is you, I hope you now feel able to do so with some confidence. Support can come in different forms. You could engage a seasoned data migration project manager to run this for you or you could engage a functional data analyst to do the hard work.

And then there are those who want to learn and undertake this journey themselves and require a little more support than a book can provide. For you, I offer data migration mentoring, let's talk about how I might help by walking alongside you every step of the way. You can get in touch at www.amandasokell.com

TECHNICAL RESOURCES

Create an OBDC Connection to Stage

1. From the Windows Start menu, select Settings-Control Panel-ODBC Data Sources (32bit).

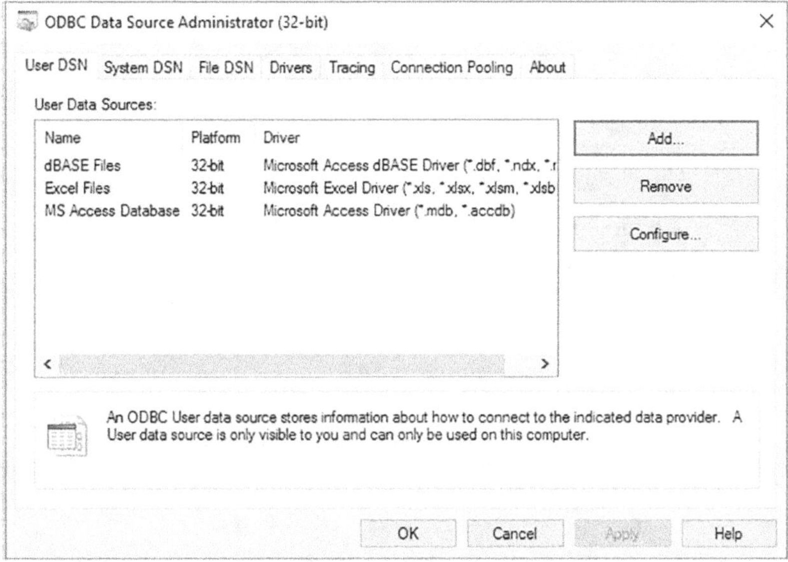

Figure 4 Windows ODBC Data Source Administrator Screen

2. Select User DSN, hit the Add button, then Select SageLine 50 v# (whatever version you are using). Hit the Finish button.

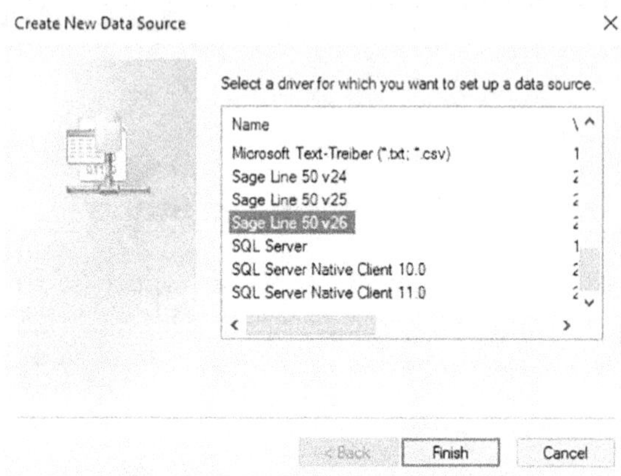

Figure 5 Windows Create New Data Source Dialog

3. A new dialog box appears. In Data Source Name type: "Demo." In the Data Path box, type: the path to your Sage Data. This can be found in Sage from Help > About.

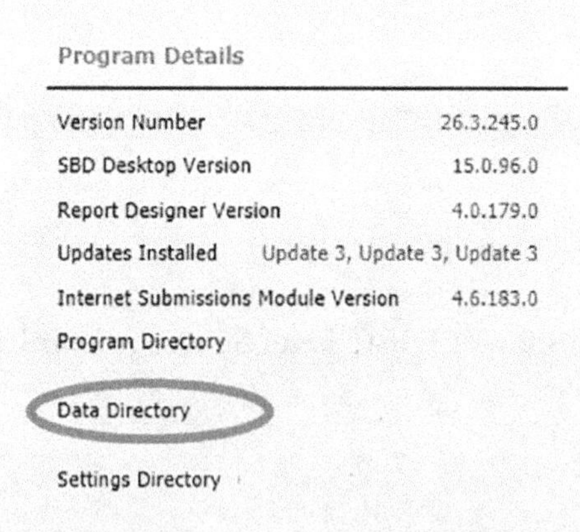

Figure 6 Sage 50 Help About Screen – Data Directory Location

4. Press OK to close the ODBC Dialog box

1. In Excel, select Data > From Other Sources > From Microsoft Query.

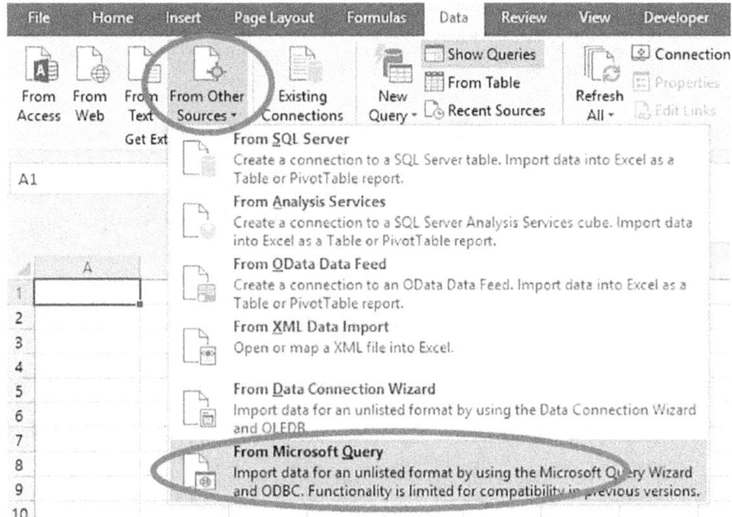

Figure 7 Excel Data Connections Menu

2. Choose your Sage ODBC Connection from the list and press OK.

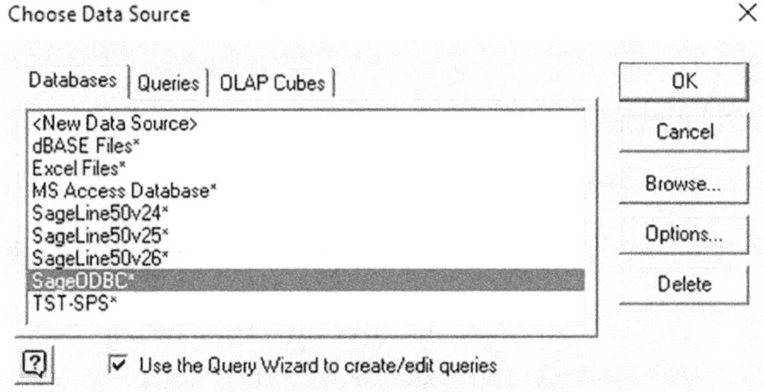

Figure 8 Microsoft Query Choose Data Source Dialog

3. Enter your Sage user ID and password and press OK.

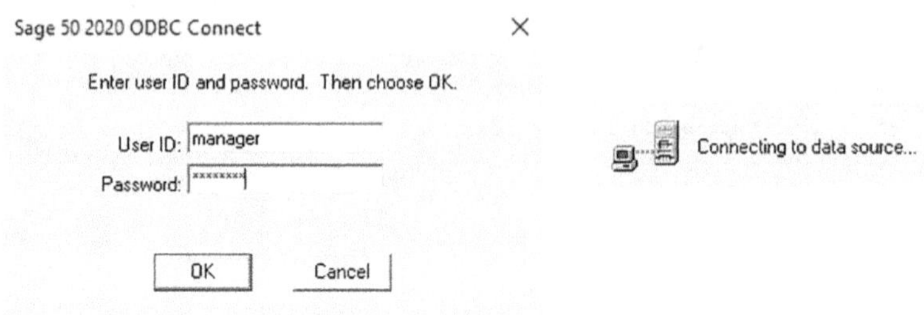

Figure 9 Microsoft Query Connection Dialog

4. You will see a list of available Sage tables in the left-hand column. Find the table containing the data you wish to review/ export. Then click on the > button to move the fields in to the right column. The image below shows the COUNTRY_ CODE table and its associated fields. Then press Next >.

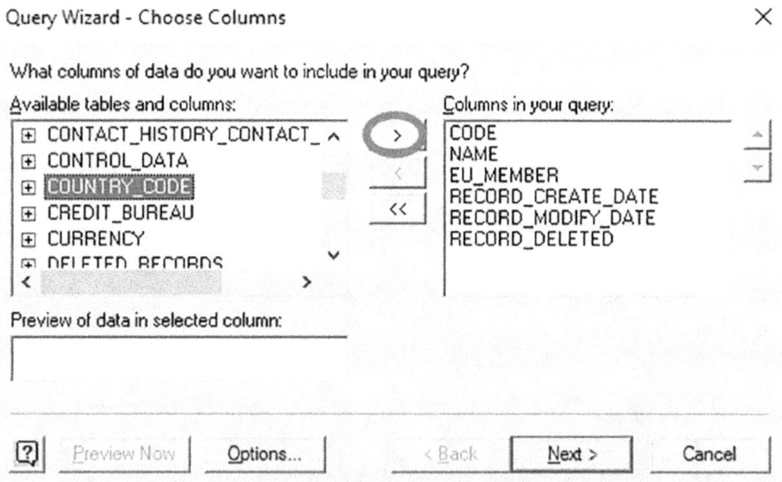

Figure 10 Microsoft Query Wizard showing
selected and available data tables/fields

5. It is generally better to pull all data and filter in Excel, so you can press Next > on the Filter screen.

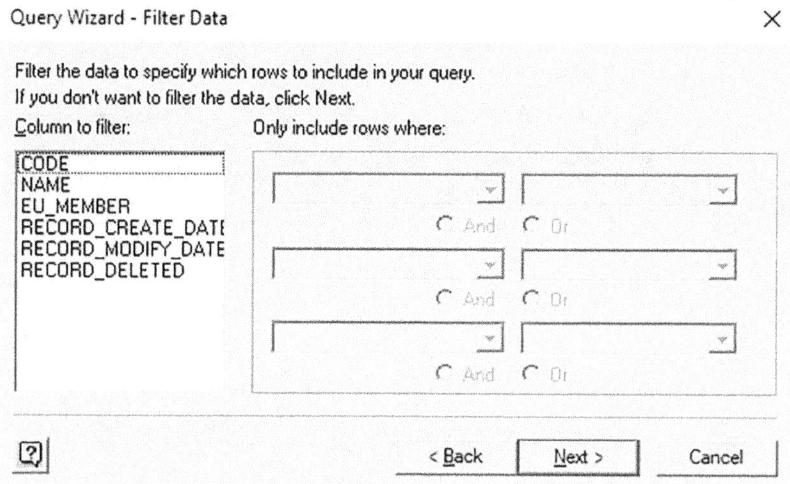

Figure 11 Microsoft Query Wizard showing filter options

6. Likewise, on the Sort screen, skip this and press Next >.

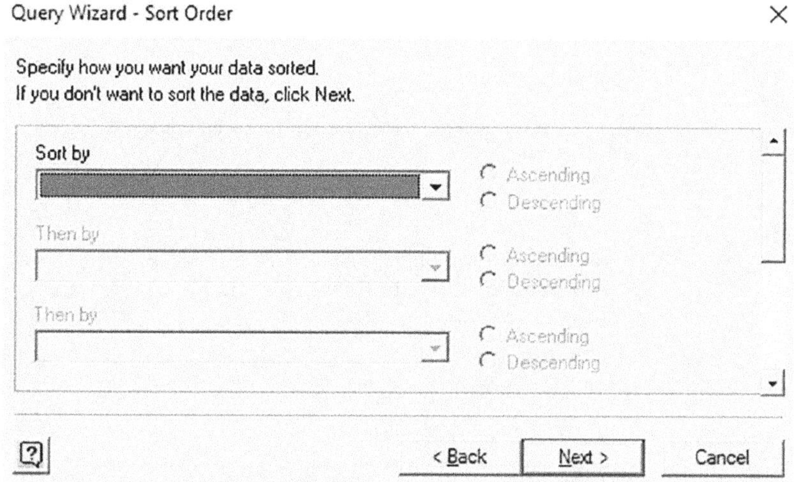

Figure 12 Microsoft Query Wizard showing sort options

7. On the Finish screen select the option to Return Data to Microsoft Excel and then press Finish.

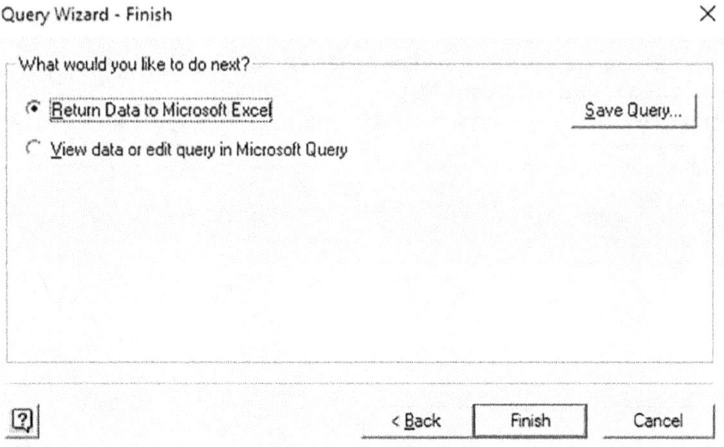

Figure 13 Microsoft Query Wizard final step

8. Select the cell where you want to place the data table. Usually, this is the top left-hand corner of a worksheet and press OK to return the data to Excel for review.

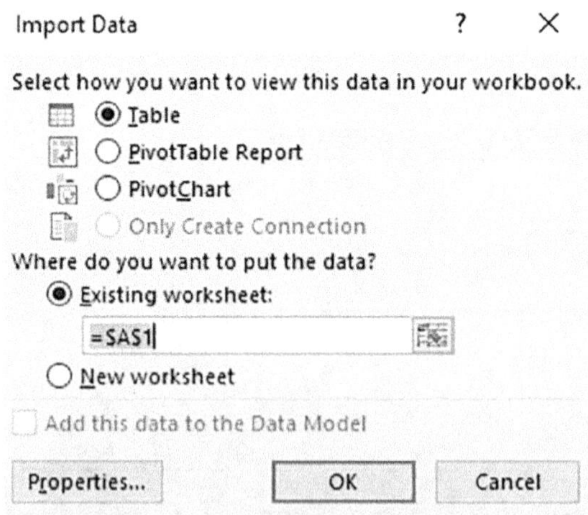

Figure 14 Microsoft Excel Import Data Dialog

Creating Multi-Key Lookup Tables

When you need to include some logic in your key structure, or any other column, Excel IF()[13] function works well.

SAGE VAT Code	Country	Key	Mapped Code
T1	UK	T1-UK	VAT20
T5	UK	T5-UK	VAT05
T0	UK	T0-UK	NOVAT
T0	AUS	T0	EXPORT
T0	USA	T0	EXPORT

The function is this:

=IF(test which returns true, value if test is true, value if test is false).

In this example:

- <test which returns true> is [Country]="UK"
- <value if test is true> = [Sage VAT CODE &"-"&[Country]
- <value if test is false> = [Sage VAT Code]

The final formula used:

Key: =If([Country]="UK",[Sage VAT Code] & "-" & [Country],[Sage VAT Code])

Using Excel Lookups

After extracting the raw data add additional columns to the right-hand side (shown here in grey). The first is the key using the same mechanism for multi-key lookup tables.

Client Name	SAGE VAT Code	Country	Key	Mapped Code
Client A	T1	UK	T1-UK	VAT20
Client B	T0	UK	T0-UK	NOVAT
Client C	T0	USA	T0	EXPORT

Then use a VLOOKUP() to get the correct mapped code. The function is this

=VLOOKUP(lookup value, range containing the lookup value, the column number in the range containing the return value, Approximate match (TRUE) or Exact match (FALSE)).

In this example:

- <lookup value> is [Key] in the Client Table
- <range containing the lookup value> is columns 3 & 4 of the Mapping table, [Key] and [Mapped Code]
- <the column number in the range containing the return value> is 2. I.e. the column [Mapped Code] is column 2 of the range, with [Key] being column 1
- <Match> will be FALSE as we want to get an exact match.

The final formula looks like this:

=VLOOKUP([@Key],_MappingTable[[Key]:[Mapped Code]],2,FALSE)

1. From an existing data table get to the query by right clicking in the table, selecting Table > Edit Query.

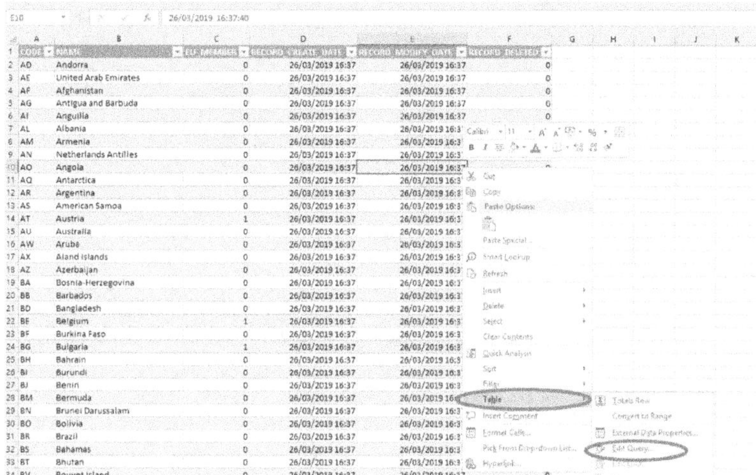

Figure 15 Microsoft Excel – Edit Existing Query Menu

2. In the Edit Query wizard, select Next until the Finish page. On this page select View data or edit query in Microsoft Query and press Finish.

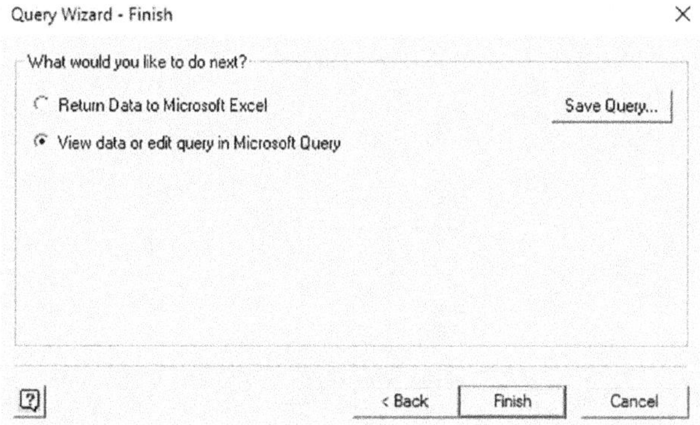

Figure 16 Microsoft Query Wizard – Edit Query Dialog

3. Press the Add table button, and select the 2nd table from the available list. Tables can only be joined if they share a common field.

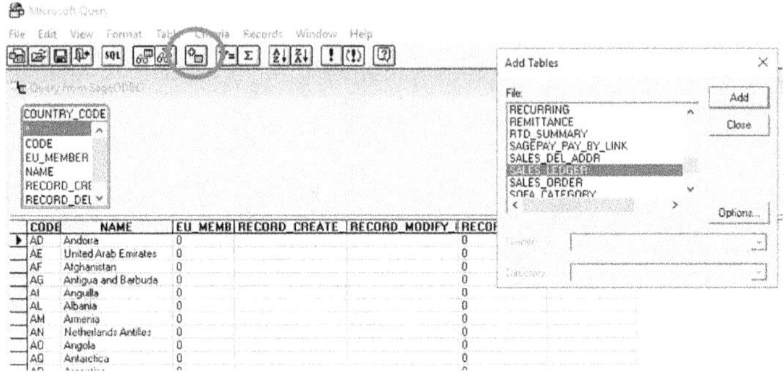

Figure 17 Microsoft Query – Add New Data Table

4. Locate the field in the 2nd table that links the two tables. Select the field in the first table, and then drag and drop it onto the corresponding field in the 2nd table. In this case CODE in the COUNTRY_CODE table links with COUNTRY_CODE in the SALES_LEDGER table.

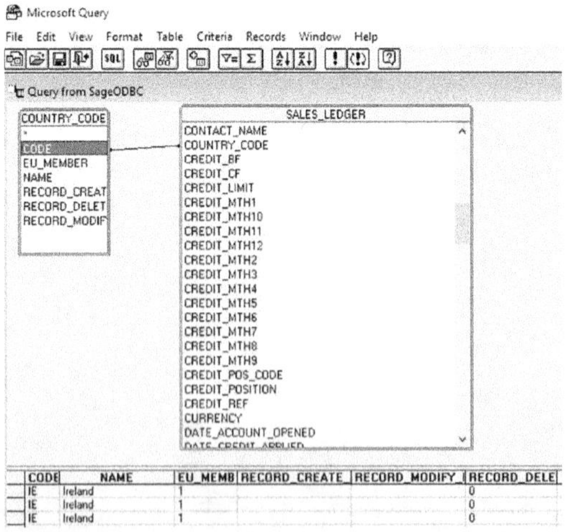

Figure 18 Microsoft Query – Join Data Tables

5. To add fields into the query, double click on the field name in the table. To remove fields from the query click on the column heading in the grid and press the DELETE button. When you have finished building the table of data Select File > Return Data to Microsoft Excel.

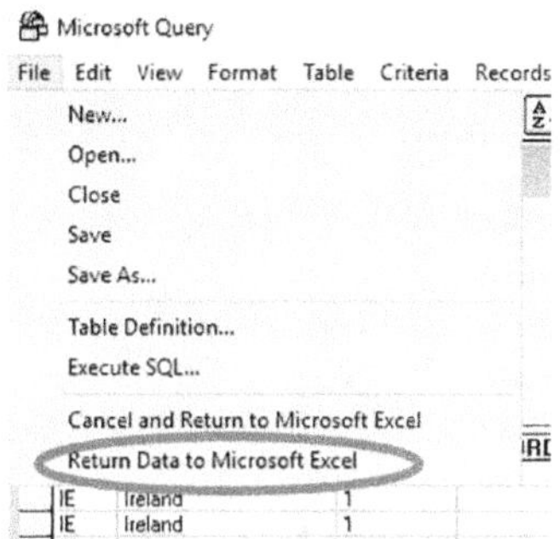

Figure 19 Microsoft Query – Return Data to Excel

Creating a Pivot Table

Let's say we want to review the country code on all our customer records.

1. Select the cell in the top left-hand corner of the data table, then select Insert > Pivot Table.

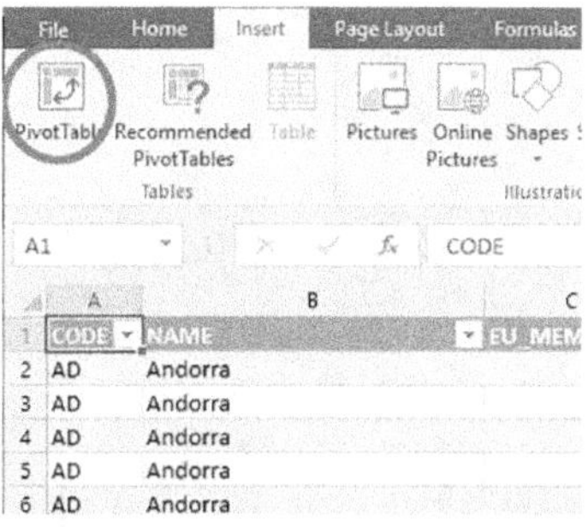

Figure 20 Microsoft Excel – Insert Pivot Table menu

2. Accept the defaults, and press OK.

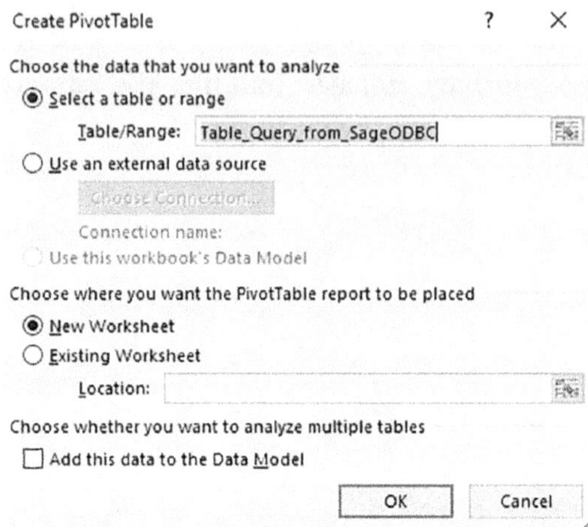

Figure 21 Microsoft Excel – Create Pivot Table Dialog

3. The Pivot Table fields are visible on the right hand side of the screen.

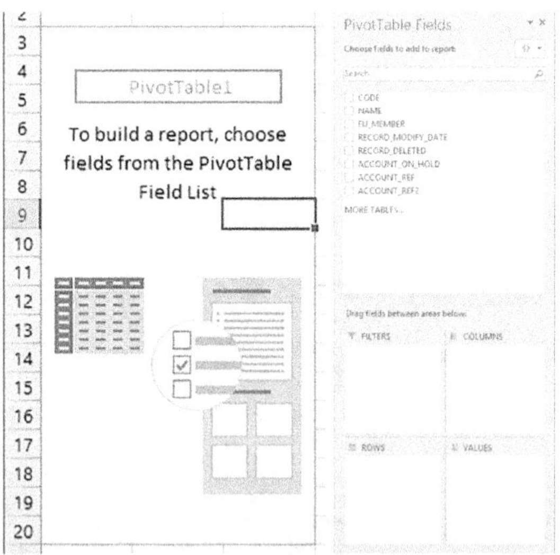

Figure 22 Microsoft Pivot Table – New Pivot Table and Pivot Fields

4. Dragging the fields into the rows will update the Pivot Table display. For example, adding the CODE and the ACCOUNT_REF you can see all the customers within each country.

Figure 23 Microsoft Excel – Pivot Table Rows

Complex Criteria

Using complex criteria, a single field can highlight the presence or absence of validation errors.

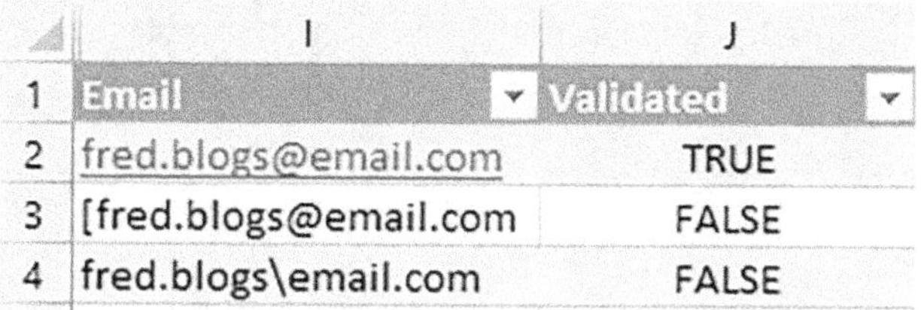

Figure 24 Microsoft Excel – Using Validation Rules to Highlight Errors

This can be achieved using the following formula:

=IF(IFERROR(FIND("@",[@Email],1),0)=0,FALSE,IF(OR
(IFERROR(FIND("\",[@Email],1),0)>0,IFERROR(FIND("[",[@
Email],1),0)>0),FALSE,TRUE)).

The structure of the formula is:

IF(<statement that is true>, 'FALSE',IF(OR(<Statement 2 that is
true>),(<statement 3 that is true>),'FALSE','TRUE')).

The <statements that are true> are expressed as looking for a string
in the email address if it can't be found returning 0. The first is testing for the absence of an @ sign. The second test is testing for the
presence of either a \ or a [. If any of these is present then validated
= TRUE.

More information on nested IF() statements can be found on the
Microsoft support site.[15]

ABOUT THE AUTHOR

Amanda Sokell creates profit from order.

She is passionate about building a world in which the right systems allow people and companies to grow. Amanda is a systems thinker, her understanding of how systems interact with each other has allowed her to successfully solve business challenges, and to improve productivity. A creative thinker and problem solver, when faced with a challenge to overcome in almost any environment, she has the skills to look at the system, the process and suggest solutions.

With a career that spans, public relations, software development, management consultancy, and training and mentoring, she has worked with businesses of all shapes and sizes from small family businesses, to global pharmaceuticals.

Amanda runs her business from Sevenoaks in Kent, where she enjoys the luxury of living at the edge of a 947-acre deer park, and finds inspiration in the breath-taking views across the downs.

She has worked on countless software projects, from the creation of systems from scratch to digital transformation projects involving moving complex businesses from one or more platforms into brand shiny new ones. Having seen the many and varied ways that data migration can go wrong, she is determined to help business leaders to understand the pitfalls, and, by following a simple road map, deliver successful digital transformation projects.

www.amandasokell.com

BIBLIOGRAPHY

[1] Bush, W T. Transforming Data - Managing the Migration: Data Migration Methodology for Managing Data in an ERP Transformation Program (Business Logic on Data Book 3)

[2] Bush, W T. Transforming Data - Managing the Migration: Data Migration Methodology for Managing Data in an ERP Transformation Program (Business Logic on Data Book 3)

[3] Morris, J. Practical Data Migration (Third edition)

[4] Information Commissioner's Office – Guide to the Data Protection [online]. Available from https://ico.org.uk/for-organisations/guide-to-data-protection/guide-to-the-general-data-protection-regulation-gdpr/key-definitions/controllers-and-processors/ [Accessed November 2020]

[5] Information Commissioner's Office – Guide to the Data Protection [online]. Available from https://ico.org.uk/for-organisations/guide-to-data-protection/guide-to-the-general-data-protection-regulation-gdpr/key-definitions/what-is-personal-data/ [Accessed November 2020]

[6] Information Commissioner's Office – Guide to the Data Protection [online]. Available from https://ico.org.uk/for-organisations/guide-to-data-protection/guide-to-the-general-data-protection-regulation-gdpr/principles/lawfulness-fairness-and-transparency/ [Accessed November 2020]

[7] Information Commissioner's Office – Guide to the Data Protection [online]. Available from https://ico.org.uk/for-organisations/guide-to-data-protection/guide-to-the-general-data-protection-regulation-gdpr/principles/purpose-limitation/ [Accessed November 2020]

8   Information Commissioner's Office – Guide to the Data Protection [online]. Available from https://ico.org.uk/for-organisations/guide-to-data-protection/guide-to-the-general-data-protection-regulation-gdpr/principles/data-minimisation/ [Accessed November 2020]

9   Information Commissioner's Office – Guide to the Data Protection [online]. Available from https://ico.org.uk/for-organisations/guide-to-data-protection/guide-to-the-general-data-protection-regulation-gdpr/principles/accuracy/ [Accessed November 2020]

10   Information Commissioner's Office – Guide to the Data Protection [online]. Available from https://ico.org.uk/for-organisations/guide-to-data-protection/guide-to-the-general-data-protection-regulation-gdpr/principles/storage-limitation/ [Accessed November 2020]

11   Information Commissioner's Office – Guide to the Data Protection [online]. Available from https://ico.org.uk/for-organisations/guide-to-data-protection/guide-to-the-general-data-protection-regulation-gdpr/security/ [Accessed November 2020]

12   Information Commissioner's Office – Guide to the Data Protection [online]. Available from https://ico.org.uk/for-organisations/guide-to-data-protection/guide-to-the-general-data-protection-regulation-gdpr/accountability-and-governance/ [Accessed November 2020]

13   Information Commissioner's Office – Guide to the Data Protection [online]. Available from https://support.microsoft.com/en-us/office/if-function-69aed7c9-4e8a-4755-a9bc-aa8bbff73be2 [Accessed November 2020]

14   Information Commissioner's Office – Guide to the Data Protection [online]. Available from https://support.microsoft.com/en-us/office/vlookup-function-0bbc8083-26fe-4963-8ab8-93a18ad188a1 [Accessed November 2020]

15   Information Commissioner's Office – Guide to the Data Protection [on-line]. Available from https://support.microsoft.com/en-us/office/if-function-%E2%80%93-nested-formulas-and-avoiding-pitfalls-0b22ff44-f149-44ba-aeb5-4ef99da241c8 [Accessed November 2020]

ACKNOWLEDGEMENTS

The inspiration for this book came from a great question posed in August 2018 by one of my mentors, Col Fink. His question was framed around, *"if you can write a book for the smallest niche possible, what would it be?"*

Having been trying for a while to work out what book was 'in me', I suddenly had inspiration, and so the idea for Migrate was born. Having the idea and writing it are however two quite different things, and after the first chapter was written the momentum quickly dried up. Thank you Col, for your continued thought provoking questions which challenge my thinking and help me to see new possibilities.

In January 2019 I found myself, unexpectedly, stranded in a ski-resort with a week to kill, having fallen on the first day of the holiday and broken my arm. Thankfully it was my left arm, and so, armed with a pen and an A4 notepad, I spent the rest of the week writing the first draft manuscript - old school. I have to thank the participants of the 2019 NetSki trip to Val D'Isere for looking after me during that week, in particular Simon West and Warren Cass the organisers, Barnaby Wynter, for the original invitation, Pollyanna English, whom I have never met, and whose place I took a week before departure and Bindar Dosanjh who was a thoughtful and helpful roomie.

This book would never have seen the light of day if it weren't for the immensely supportive community at Thought Leaders Business School. Writing a book is something many people never consider, let alone achieve. The TLBS community makes writing a book, not just normal, but expected, and without that expectation, I'm not sure I would have had the courage to get this far. Thank you in particular to Matt Church, Peter Cook and Lisa O'Neill for creating such a powerful community.

This book is possible, largely as a result of the many clients who have entrusted me, over the years, to provide them with help, advice, and practical support with their own data migrations. If I try to name you all, it is inevitable I will forget someone. Instead, as you know who you are, please understand your trust with such a precious asset of your business was a privilege.

I should also like to thank the various IT professionals who took the time to provide me with their perspective on data migration. Thank you for taking the time to give me an insight into the problems you experience and how this book might help you and others solve them. Special thanks to Richard Thompson, Simon Mendoza, Andy Knap, Colin Scott, Gerry Lawrence, Nigel Slone and Steve Stovold among others.

I'm grateful for the time taken by David Saunders of Kingsline Solutions and Robert Burbidge to help me understand how quickly address data becomes out of date, the various reasons why this might happen and how companies can keep their data up to date. You both shared far more information than I eventually included, and I hope that readers will seek you out, or approach your industry colleagues for advice on how the data in their new systems, can stay as current as possible.

Becoming a writer when you feel your strengths lie in other areas, is a daunting prospect. I have never thought of myself as somebody who can write prose that others would choose to read. Part of the process for me has been to spend months and months writing weekly blogs. My thanks go in particular to another, long standing mentor, Chris Hughes, for his unfailing support in not only reading my weekly epistles but replying and telling me what he liked about them. Chris, you have helped give me the confidence to publish this book.

Thanks also go to my beta readers, Trevor Sokell, Chris Bose and Rachel Gooen. Dad, your feedback was honest and only a parent could get away with it. Chris and Rachel, thank you for not being a relative. If I'd stuck with one beta reader we wouldn't be here now.

Finally, and most importantly of all, I need to thank my family. To my husband Ian, for giving me the space to do my thing, without pressure or recrimination when things haven't necessarily gone the right way. Over many years you have supported me as and when required, emotionally, financially and practically. And to our two sons, Alex and Felix whose questions about life, learning and what mum does for a living have kept us all entertained.

www.ingramcontent.com/pod-product-compliance
Lightning Source LLC
Chambersburg PA
CBHW060939050726
47592CB00003B/1019